Digitalization, Technology and Global Business

Gaston Fornes • Maria Altamira

Digitalization, Technology and Global Business

How Technology is Shaping Value
Creation Across Borders

palgrave
macmillan

Gaston Fornes
University of Bristol Business School
University of Bristol
Bristol, UK

Maria Altamira
UBI Business School
Brussels, Belgium

ISBN 978-3-031-33110-7   ISBN 978-3-031-33111-4   (eBook)
https://doi.org/10.1007/978-3-031-33111-4

This Palgrave Pivot imprint is published by the registered company Springer Nature Switzerland AG.
The registered company address is: Gewerbestrasse 11, 6330 Cham, Switzerland

To our parents, an endless source of good examples and inspiration. Thanks.
To Chloe and Mateo, for the light they bring every day.

Contents

About the Authors

Maria Altamira holds a PhD from the University of Warwick (UK) and is Senior Fellow of the Higher Education Academy. Her area of expertise is internationalization and innovation strategies of Chinese multinationals. Maria Altamira started her professional career at Accenture in 2007 where she was a Strategic Consultant specialized in customer relationship management, strategic marketing, and innovation in the high technology industry. In 2011, she began to be professionally involved in business and projects in China. She is developing her professional career in higher education with a focus on international strategy and development and academic quality.

Gaston Fornes completed his post-doctoral studies at IE Business School (Spain) after receiving a PhD in Management from the University of Bath (UK) and is Principal Fellow of the Higher Education Academy. Gaston Fornes started his professional career at Citibank and then funded what became a mid-sized company with operations in Chile and Argentina. In the past 20 years, he has combined academic and executive responsibilities. During this period, he has been highly involved professionally with China where, for his work with SMEs, he received the

Liupan Mountain Friendship Award from the Ningxia Government for his "contribution to Ningxia's economy and society". He has also received the Foreign Expert Award from the Shanghai Government and was awarded the London School of Economics—Latin American Development Bank Fellowship. Gaston Fornes has been featured in mass media such as CGTN, *Fortune*, RFI, the BBC, TN, *El Pais* or *Cinco Dias*.

List of Figures

List of Boxes

1

Introduction

Abstract This chapter sets the context and agenda for the discussion in the book and frames the key elements that impact both international business and digitalization/technology. Different angles and perspectives are introduced, building upon mainstream theoretical frameworks, discussions, and primary and secondary research. As technology-enabled transformation in a globalized market is imperative to maintain growth, the book intends to develop a deep understanding of the current environment and of possible future scenarios necessary to keep growth and therefore propel businesses forward.

Keywords Globalization • Digitalization • Technology

"The Web as I envisaged it, we have not seen it yet. The future is still so much bigger than the past"
—Tim Berners-Lee, inventor of the World Wide Web *(Computer History Museum, 2022)*

© The Author(s), under exclusive license to Springer Nature Switzerland AG 2023
G. Fornes, M. Altamira, *Digitalization, Technology and Global Business*,
https://doi.org/10.1007/978-3-031-33111-4_1

1.1   Motivation

Starting a book by saying that the world has changed and continues changing is not new. What is new though is the need to have a deep understanding and insights on the impacts that these changes are having in the way international businesses are run and grown. The main changes in recent years have come from the ubiquitous presence of technology in our daily life (and therefore in business) and also by the direction globalization has taken. The former can be seen in the way companies develop their competitive capabilities to support their growth; from the Industrial Revolution and during much of the 20th century the focus was on the development of capabilities for products and manufacturing; then with the arrival of the internet the focus moved to services and their provision; now the focus is on developing capabilities that lead to technology-based business models. This focus on the management of technology, understood as the planning, development, and implementation of technological capabilities to shape and accomplish both the strategic and operational objectives of the organization (Li-Hua, 2007), is expected to be the main competitive ground for at least the next ten years.

In fact, technology is behind the changes in globalization. Since the end of the Cold War international trade and foreign investments have been growing at record rates (Fornes & Mendez, 2018), even the 2007–2008 global financial crisis, the trade disputes between China and the USA during the Trump presidency, or the Covid pandemic did not reduce their growth (Altman & Bastian, 2021). But this is now changing, the world seems to be divided into two trade and political blocks, each fueled by the intention and ambition to dominate the technology that will run the economy in the future (Financial Times Reporters, 2022; Wolf, 2022) (digital sovereignty is explained in Chap. 6). This means that companies need to review their sources of growth, especially if the barriers to international trade, investments, and technology transfer are raised. This is the main motivation of this book: we want (i) to critically analyze the impact of digitalization and technology on incumbent international business theories, (ii) to deeply understand how digitalization and technology can create (more) growth opportunities, (iii) to engage with the opportunities and challenges that digital models and new technologies, digital platforms and Artificial Intelligence in particular, are bringing to the current business and economic environment, and (iv) to think of possible scenarios and trends that can be the source of growth in the future. We expect this book to bring implications for practitioners, policymakers, and academics.

1.2   Context

Digitalization and technology-based business have been the main driver of growth for companies and industries since the beginning of the century; in fact, in the last 15 years the fastest growing companies have been those with technology-based business models. In addition, companies like Alphabet/Google, Apple, Meta/Facebook, Microsoft, or Amazon have taken the top positions as the world's most valuable enterprises, replacing in these spots long standing firms like GE, ExxonMobil, or Coca-Cola (Statista, 2022a). Growth opportunities due to technological developments are expected to continue. The Word Economic Forum (2022) forecasts that 70% of new value created globally over the next 10 years will be based on digital and technology-based business models. In 2023, for the first time, more than half of GDP will be driven by 'digitally transformed' enterprises (Statista, 2022b). In this sense, PWC (2017) projected that gains from Artificial Intelligence alone will contribute $15.7 trillion to the global economy by 2030; major innovation trends that underpin these developments include Web3, Industry 5.0, Supply Chain 4.0, and 5G (Startup Genome, 2022). In addition, the pandemic has challenged the status quo and conventional thinking across all industries and as a result these timeframes are accelerating.

Most of these forecasts assumed that the current state of globalization would continue in more or less the same shape as in the past 20-30 years. They were based on what has been defined as 'digital globalization', a context where nations, industries, people, and firms are connected through 'flows of data information, ideas, and knowledge, [as well as] through flows of goods, services, investments, and capital that are digitally enabled or supported' (Luo, 2021, p. 1). These flows are supported by ubiquitous technologies like data analytics, cloud services, internet, or ICT; and most of the trade and transactions take place in digital platforms like online or e-commerce marketplaces. As technology-enabled transformation in a globalized market is imperative to maintain growth, a deep understanding of the current environment and of possible future scenarios is necessary to maintain growth and therefore propel businesses forward (GHD, 2022).

The first step for this understanding is the recognition that many companies and industries are still having difficulties to deeply engage with digitalization and the management of technology to support their growth. For example in Europe, one of the world's most advanced economies, the European Commission (2022) has found that over 70% of businesses still lack the digital and technology management skills required for investment and growth, and also it estimates that over 805,000 digital leaders will be needed by 2025. In this context, Julian Lamertin of KRC Research, who assisted Microsoft with the Future of Work report, expressed that there will be a point in the future when all the technology has been built and the demand for software programmers and data scientists will deplete (Hill, 2022); however, what is needed is people who can work with technology and apply their interpersonal and leadership skills.

The second and probably more important step for this understanding is the recognition that both globalization and technology development are intertwined, and both have changed the business environment by providing firms with the means to respond to this change fast. For example, 'it took 1,000 years for the invention of paper to spread from China to Europe. Nowadays, in a world that has become more integrated, innovations spread faster and through many channels' (Aslam et al., 2018). Technological developments do not happen everywhere or at the same time, although they are the main pillar to improve living standards; therefore, knowledge flows facilitated by globalization have been key to generate global growth. This has been because companies located in different countries have had easy access to foreign knowledge, and also because this has increased international competition (mainly due to the rise of companies based in emerging economies) which as a consequence has created a strong incentive to keep innovating. In this context, one type of beneficiary has been emerging markets-based firms as they have increased their participation in global supply chains with multinational companies (Aslam et al., 2018). If the world continues in the direction of having two trade blocks, it is highly likely knowledge flows will be limited and therefore global growth hindered (and probably growth will be more concentrated in technology leading countries).

1.3 Rationale, Definitions, and Structure

The book is structured to present the key elements that impact both international business and digitalization/technology. Different angles and perspectives have been taken, building upon mainstream theoretical frameworks, discussions, and primary and secondary research to analyze the current state of the literature; these perspectives and angles are then supported by examples and applications. For this purpose, we have used the following two definitions of digitalization and being/becoming digital. The former, digitalization, is basically operational, seeking to standardize processes and optimize operations through the use of different technologies and software. The latter, being/becoming digital, means the use of digital technologies to articulate, target, and personalize alternative offers in order to define a new value proposition (Aagaard, 2019; Sebastian et al., 2020). Throughout the book we use being/becoming digital, management of technology, and technology-based business interchangeably.

In this context, Chapter 2, *The Digital and International Business: a historical perspective*, presents a critical review of mainstream theories of international business and how they have developed over time (more than 50 years) to accommodate the increasing digitalization of companies along with the higher prevalence of technology-based businesses. Chapter 3, *Internationalization, Digitalization, and Exponential Growth*, continues this analysis and incorporates growth as a key variable. A literature review of the field is developed along with a deep critical analysis of the application of mainstream internationalization theories to explain the impact of digitalization and technologies on the firm's accelerated and/or exponential international growth, with almost instant access to overseas markets.

This is followed by Chap. 4, *Platforms and International Business*, where digital platforms that have become the main pillar for the exchange of information, services and goods are analyzed. The focus of the analysis is on how these platforms, a relatively recent phenomenon, are impacting the international expansion of companies and therefore growth. It analyzes how platforms have allowed companies to reach wider markets in a fast and efficient manner, with a special reflection about their impact on the international expansion of Small and Medium Enterprises (SMEs). Chapter 5, *Artificial Intelligence and International Business*, takes a more practical approach and develops a critical analysis of the impact this new technology is having on today's business context and society and of how it is contributing to enhance the competitive position of firms around the globe. Challenges and the future of Artificial Intelligence are also discussed.

Chapter 6, *Data Management and Regulations for International Business*, discusses the current regulatory framework for data management, and critically assesses the challenges presented by a fragmented and incomplete system and future needs to ensure a fair use of data across models, which will, in turn, support a sustainable growth of technology-based business models. Every chapter includes an application and discussion section in which real cases and experiences are analyzed to support and illustrate the arguments developed about the topic. Finally, the book concludes with Chap. 7, *Conclusions, Challenges, and Trends*, with a recap and a discussion of future challenges and possible scenarios.

References

Aagaard, A. (Ed.). (2019). *Digital business models. Driving transformation and innovation*. Palgrave Macmillan.

Altman, S., & Bastian, C. (2021). The state of globalization in 2021. *Harvard Business Review*. Retrieved from https://hbr.org/2021/03/the-state-of-globalization-in-2021

Aslam, A., Eugster, J., Ho, G., Jaumotte, F., Osorio-Buitron, C., & Piazza, R. (2018). Globalization helps spread knowledge and technology across borders. Retrieved from https://www.imf.org/en/Blogs/Articles/2018/04/09/globalization-helps-spread-knowledge-and-technology-across-borders.

Computer History Museum. (2022). Fellowship for Prof Tim Berners-Lee for his seminal contributions to the development of the World Wide Web. Retrieved from https://computerhistory.org/profile/tim-berners-lee/

Financial Times Reporters. (2022). How the US chip export controls have turned the screws on China. *Financial Times*. Retrieved from https://www.ft.com/content/bbbdc7dc-0566-4a05-a7b3-27afd82580f3.

Fornes, G., & Mendez, A. (2018). *The China-Latin America Axis. Emerging markets and their role in an increasingly globalised world*. Palgrave Macmillan.

GHD. (2022). Ten emerging trends shaping our new future. Retrieved from https://www.ghd.com/en/perspectives/ten-emerging-trends-shaping-our-new-future.aspx

Li-Hua, R. (2007). What is technology management? *Journal of Technology Management in China, 2*(1), 1. https://doi.org/10.1108/jtmc.2007.30202aaa.001

Luo, Y. (2021). New OLI advantages in digital globalization. *International Business Review, 30*, 1. https://doi.org/10.1016/j.ibusrev.2021.101777

PWC. (2017). Sizing the prize. PWC's Global Artificial Intelligence Study: Exploiting the AI Revolution. Retrieved from https://www.pwc.com/gx/en/issues/analytics/assets/pwc-ai-analysis-sizing-the-prize-report.pdf

Sebastian, I., Ross, J., Beath, C., Mocker, M., Moloney, K., & Fonstad, N. (2020). How big old companies navigate digital transformation. In R. Galliers, D. Leidner, & B. Simeonova (Eds.), *Strategic information management. Theory and practice* (5th ed.). Routledge.

Startup Genome. (2022). The global startup ecosystem report. Retrieved from https://startupgenome.com/es/article/the-state-of-the-global-startup-economy

Statista. (2022a). The 100 largest companies in the world by market capitalization in 2022. Retrieved from https://www.statista.com/statistics/263264/top-companies-in-the-world-by-market-capitalization/

Statista. (2022b). GDP Driven by digital transformation 2018–2023. Retrieved from https://www.statista.com/statistics/1134766/nominal-gdp-driven-by-digitally-transformed-enterprises/

Word Economic Forum. (2022). These are the top 10 job skills of tomorrow – and how long it takes to learn them. Retrieved from https://www.weforum.org/agenda/2020/10/top-10-work-skills-of-tomorrow-how-long-it-takes-to-learn-them/

2

The Digital Economy and International Business, an Historical Perspective

Abstract The chapter critically analyzes the mainstream internationalization theories, starting from those developed in the West in the second part of the last century and continuing with those developed for emerging markets-based firms that appeared at the beginning of the 21st century. The focus of the discussion is the explanatory power of these theories in a highly digitalized environment. In this context, while some authors argue that the analytical approach of internationalization theories is still valid, it has been recognized that there are some elements that need to be revised to fully capture the impact of digitalization and new technologies. In particular, it seems that theories would need to be adapted so they can better explain how the following consequences of digitalization are influencing the international expansion of firms: (i) A reduction of transaction costs, (ii) an increase of network economies, speed, and scalability, (iii) the changing nature of firm-specific advantages and capabilities, (iv) the new definition of MNEs and the idea of digitally networked ecosystems, (v) the place/location moving from physical and territorial attributes, to digital and information flow-based attributes, and finally (vi) the different price settings.

Keywords Internationalization theories • Explanatory power • Digital economy

> *"We are very lucky because the world is in a big transformation because of technology. This new technology will create a lot of successful people, interesting careers but honestly every new technology will create social problems."*
> —Jack Ma, Founder of Alibaba, *(Ma, 2018)*

2.1 Introduction

This chapter presents a critical review of mainstream international business theories and how they have developed over time (more than 60 years) to accommodate the increasing digitalization of companies along with the higher prevalence of technology-based business. It starts with the rationale of how mainstream theories were developed mainly through the research of firms from Western economies expanding overseas. It continues with an analysis of emerging markets-based firms as companies from these markets started to be relevant players in foreign direct investments after the mid-2000s (in fact, Chinese companies have been the second largest foreign investor for the last eight years (UNCTAD, 2022)). The chapter concludes with a critical analysis of digitalization and internationalization theories, with the focus on how they can (still) explain the international expansion of companies in an environment that has changed dramatically due to the adoption of technologies.

2.2 Internationalization Theories and the Digital Economy

Antecedents of Mainstream Theories [1]

Foreign direct investment (FDI) theory developed in the late 1960s and 1970s (Caves, 1971, 1974; Hymer, 1960, 1968; McManus, 1972; Vernon, 1966, 1974), basically by adding a cross-border/geographical diversification to the theory of the firm to explain the activities of companies outside their national boundaries financed by FDI. Also during the same time, studies on multinational enterprises became increasingly interdisciplinary with organizational or behavioral studies making increasingly important contributions. This was triggered mainly by the poor view of the traditional profit-maximizing company during the 1960s, and by a realization of the importance of the way firms were organized to perform their value-added activities (Dunning, 2003)

In the 1970s, Buckley and Casson (1976) in "The Future of the Multinational Enterprise", identified a juxtaposition of two strands of economic theory with the firm as the main unit of analysis which then became one of the dominant conceptual frameworks on the multinational enterprise. First, by looking at the firm as an exchange function, Buckley and Casson analyzed why firms internalize product markets and, by doing so, how they benefit from a reduction of transaction costs [2]. Second, by analyzing the company as a value-adding unit, they examined the tasks/transformation functions that are unique to the firm and add value in a cost-effective way (tasks/functions that the market cannot undertake). The combination of these exchange and value-adding functions determines the profitability of the company along with its growth prospects. Figure 2.1 shows the theoretical developments upon which Buckley and Casson's framework is based.

---

[1] Adapted from Fornes (2009).

[2] Defined as "the costs of specifying and enforcing the contracts that underlie exchange and therefore comprise all the costs of political and economic organization that permit economies to capture the gains from trade" (North, 1984, p. 7).

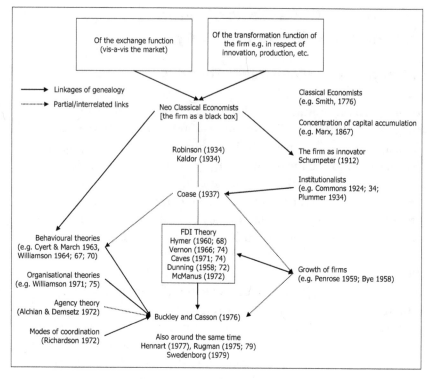

Fig. 2.1 Some antecedents of internationalization theory. (Adapted from Dunning, 2003)

At around the same time that Buckley and Casson presented their work, Dunning (1977) developed what is known as the OLI paradigm or the eclectic theory. This theory is, in the words of the author, a second stage of enquiry on international business, trying to offer a more integrated approach on the why, where, and how of internationalization activities. As with the Buckley and Casson model, the OLI theory is also a juxtaposition but, in this case, of three interrelated factors rather than of two strands of economic theory. The three factors are: (i) "the competitive (or O specific) advantages of existing or potential MNEs (inter alia as identified by the resource-based, evolutionary, and organizational theories of the firm), (ii) the locational (or L specific) advantages of particular countries in offering complementary assets, for these advantages to be exploited or augmented, and (iii) the propensity of the firms possessing the O specific advantages to combine these with those foreign-based assets, by FDI, rather than by (or in addition to) the market mechanism or some kind of non-equity cooperative venture" (Dunning, 2001b, p. 43) (Box 2.1).

The years from the late 1980s to 2000 saw some new and other complementary explanations to theories of international business activity in addition to a trend of multidisciplinary research. During this period,

Box 2.1 Criticism of Dunning's OLI paradigm

Dunning (2001a) has recognized criticisms of the OLI paradigm in four different areas. First, of the claim that the "explanatory variables identified by the paradigm are so numerous that its predictive value is almost zero", Dunning said that each OLI variable included in the paradigm is based on "economic or organizational theory", that the paradigm's objective is to offer a set of variables to satisfactorily explain the "particular types of foreign value-added activity", and that, for this reason, similar criticism could be applied to other "general theories of FDI and MNE activity". Second, to the suggestion that "it is misleading to suggest that the triumvirate of variables which make up the eclectic paradigm are independent of one another", Dunning stated that "it is the successful coordination of the O advantages of foreign and domestic firms with their own L advantages, and how each affects and is affected by the modality of resource deployment, that determines the extent to which a particular country is able to sustain, or upgrade its wealth-creating capacities over a period of time" (Dunning, 2001a).

The third area of criticism implied that "the eclectic paradigm insufficiently allows for differences in the strategic response of firms to any given configuration of OLI variables" and that "the paradigm is couched in static (or comparatively static) terms and offers little guidance as to the dynamics of the internationalization process of firms". Dunning responded by saying that "the strategy followed by firms in response to a given OLI configuration in time t_0 is governed by their desire to protect or influence that configuration in t_1". Finally, Kojima (1982) presented a fourth criticism of the eclectic paradigm by saying that Dunning's approach, "and that of the internationalization scholars, is purely a micro-economic phenomenon" (Dunning, 2001a, p. 180). Dunning found that these arguments fall down as Kojima "insists upon applying a strictly neo-classical framework of thought to explain a phenomenon that is outside that framework of thought".

three main strands of thinking were recognized (Dunning, 2001b). The first strand argued that companies go abroad or increase their international operations to improve their competitive advantages, to create new advantages, and to exploit these advantages (Chen & Chen, 1998; Dunning, 1996; Dunning & Lundan, 1998; Enright, 1998, 2000; Kogut & Zander, 1994; Kuemmerle, 1999; Malmberg et al., 1996; Moon, 1999; Solvell & Birkinshaw, 2000; Wesson, 1993, 1997). The second thread focused its research on the forms taken by foreign investments, a strand fueled mainly by the wave of mergers, acquisitions, joint ventures, alliances, etc. which occurred during the two decades (Casson, 2000; Kogut & Kulatilaka, 1994). The third strand looked at the inclusion of international non-equity cooperative agreements in the field of international economic involvement to: (i) help firms improve their R&D capabilities, (ii) use resources and skills available in different parts of the world and coordinate with those internally controlled, and (iii) benefit from taking part in clusters (Doz et al., 1997; Dunning, 1995; Florida, 1995; Storper & Scott, 1995) (Box 2.2 and Box 2.3).

Box 2.2 The Resource-Based View and internationalization[3]

Most works in this area, framed within the Resource-Based View (RBV) (Barney, 1991; Penrose, 1959), have analyzed the complementary resources and/or capabilities that firms deploy in their international expansion processes (Barney et al., 2001; Conner & Prahalad, 1996), capabilities that firms already have and which cannot be transferred without high costs (Barney, 1991). For example, one of the firm-specific complementary resources considered by RBV is the international experience (Barney et al., 2001) that is built and accumulated from dealing with clients, competitors, and suppliers overseas (Camison & Villar-Lopez, 2010).

This knowledge is unique to a particular company and therefore cannot be easily acquired, assimilated, replicated, or applied (Zheng & Qu, 2015). As such, it can support the development of new resources and capabilities difficult to obtain by competitors due to the high cost of developing, acquiring, or using that knowledge. Moreover, organizational learning gained through previous internationalization experiences can support the

(continued)

---

[3] Adapted from Fornes and Cardoza (2019).

Box 2.2 continued

development of new capabilities that ultimately influence the firm's performance (Delios & Beamish, 2001). However, the acquisition and internalization of this knowledge and the absorption of these competencies require a carefully designed learning strategy and commitment by the firm.

This organizational learning "enhances firms' understanding about culture, institutions, and market characteristics in the local markets" (Zheng & Qu, 2015, p. 56) and as a consequence offers the ability to adapt to local customers' specific requirements (Calhoun, 2002; Cavusgil & Zou, 1994). Following this line of reasoning, companies that have not had enough time to acquire this knowledge (mainly those at an early stage of their international expansion) face liability of foreignness, liability of newness, liability of expansion, and liability of outsidership as they lack information, relationship partners, and complementary resources (Cuervo-Cazurra et al., 2007; Johanson & Vahlne, 2009).

Box 2.3 Institutions and internationalization[4]

The institutional environment (IE), defined as the "set of fundamental political, social, and legal ground rules that establishes the basis for production, exchange, and distribution" (Davis & North, 1971, p. 6), is developed to structure and coordinate political, economic, and social relationships among members of a given society. Institutions are essential for economic development (North, 1991; Williamson, 1985) to reduce the uncertainty and transaction costs derived from imperfect information (North, 1993, 1995). The institutional environment is formed by formal institutions like regulatory frameworks, laws, or standards, and informal institutions like norms, values, or practices (North, 1990).

The international business literature has shown that IE affects companies' performance due to cultural distance (Hofstede, 1981; Kogut & Singh, 1988), unfamiliarity with business conditions (or liability of foreignness) (Fornes & Cardoza, 2018; Johanson & Vahlne, 1977; Zaheer, 1995), different public policies, legal institutions, and regulatory structures (Davis & North, 1971; Kittilaksanawong, 2017; Peng et al., 2005), among other factors. In this context, research has shown that institutions matter, but what is relevant to know is *how* institutions matter (Peng et al., 2008) to: (i) get useful insights for companies' strategy design and decision-making processes; (ii) evaluate strategic options for national and international expansion, and (iii) design, implement, and evaluate public policies to promote firms' expansion (Khanna & Palepu, 2010; Mathews, 2018).

---

[4] Adapted from Fornes et al. (2021).

Emerging Markets Multinationals[5]

Since 2000, studies have been looking to understand the sources of international competitiveness of firms from emerging markets. These companies started to internationalize their operations seeking markets abroad, in particular after China joined the WTO in 2001. Several works (framed within the RBV) found that the majority of the firms' ownership advantages supporting their international expansion were home country specific and also based on the development of local networks (see, for example, Altamira (2021); Boisot and Meyer (2008); Deng (2011); Rugman and Li (2007); Zhou (2007)) rather than the firm-specific advantages/capabilities on which incumbent MNCs support their growth across borders (Buckley & Casson, 1976; Dunning, 2003).

To complement these studies, Mathews (2006) brought forward Linkage–Leverage–Learning (LLL) as an extension of the OLI paradigm (Dunning, 2003), arguing that the internationalization of firms from emerging markets [6] needs to be reconceived as a combination of an external 'pull' (from international consumers and firms) along with an internal strategic 'push' from the company. Linkage means entering into collaborative partnerships in international markets to access and benefit from external strategic resources (as these companies usually did not have strong ownership advantages). Leverage reflects the firms' capacity to use these external resources to share knowledge across the network; like technology licensing contracts, imitation, reverse engineering, etc. And Learning includes the capacity of the company to learn by doing (rather than developing internal capabilities and then expanding internationally), as well as the repeated application of the linkage and leverage processes that lead to organizational learning.

In addition to the internal capabilities focus (related to the RBV and LLL), the institutional environment in emerging markets has also received

---

[5] Adapted from Fornes and Butt Philip (2014).
[6] Mathews worked in the Asia Pacific region, but subsequent works have shown that it can also be applied to companies from other emerging regions.

a large amount of attention[7] to understand the performance of these companies. This is because EMs present a relatively weak institutional environment (Buckley et al., 2018; Hoskisson et al., 2000), weaknesses that are tangible in three main areas: (i) lack of relevant information: comprehensive, reliable, and objective information to make decisions is not always widely available; (ii) misguided regulations: political goals are sometimes prioritized over economic efficiency reducing thus the chances to take full advantage of business opportunities and, (iii) inefficient legal systems: independent judicial systems enforcing contracts reliably and predictably are not always present in EMs (Fornes & Mendez, 2018; Khanna & Palepu, 1997; Khanna & Palepu, 2010).

These institutional voids are translated mainly into higher transaction costs and market failures which are evident in relatively poorly developed capital and labor markets (Cardoza et al., 2016) which usually result in EM-based firms being forced to internalize market functions (Buckley et al., 2018; Child & Rodrigues, 2005; Khanna & Palepu, 2000; Vassolo et al., 2011). Because the price system does not provide reliable information for the efficient allocation of resources, and governments' discretion, rather than the rule of law, determines property rights (Wright et al., 2005), firms face institutional barriers in their business expansion. In this sense, North (2005) argued that this uncertainty originates primarily in informal institutions because of the opaqueness and/or incommensurability of practices, values, or norms and their effect on decision-making.

To face the challenges of a weak IE, informal institutions (for example, in the form of relations, alliances, or networks) help companies to overcome market failures by getting access to capital, sometimes at below-market rates or subsidized/soft loans (Buckley et al., 2007; Vassolo et al., 2011), by accessing state-supported research and capital (Shi et al., 2017; Zeng & Williamson, 2003), or by protecting operations from domestic and international competitors (Buckley, 2018; Hoskisson et al., 2000). Informal institutions also assist in reducing transaction costs by, for instance, creating mechanisms for improving access to market information, firms matching, and referral (Rauch & Trindade, 2002; Suseno & Pinnington, 2018), by expanding the market and deepening competitive

---

[7] Adapted from Fornes et al. (2021).

positioning (Estrin & Prevezer, 2011; Park & Luo, 2001; Ruan, 2017), by improving the engagement with trade associations located in the destination market (Brache & Felzensztein, 2019), by creating trust-based bonds (Goel & Karri, 2006), or by strengthening/undermining corporate governance (Estrin & Prevezer, 2011; Karhunen et al., 2018).

Digitalization and Internationalization Theories

Also from the 2000s, several studies have been seeking to understand the impact of digitalization on extant theories. After a review of the different streams, Narula et al. (2019) asserted that the analytical approach of internationalization theories is still valid to explain the strategic choices of different types of MNEs even if it was originally developed to understand the appearance of advanced economies-based firms after WWII. However, they recognized new emerging themes in the transaction costs associated with the combination of assets in different environments as well as new forms of ownership, control, and responsibility. In addition, Hennart (2019) implied that most of the impact of digitalization depends on the firm's business model rather than on its internationalization strategy (as, for example, digital business models can be easily copied by competitors) and also because the international transfer of some digital business models is difficult and sometimes impossible due to the differences between home- and host-country regulations (Pollman & Barry, 2017).

Petricevic and Teece (2019, p. 1504) analyzed the movements in the international economy and added that the increasing interventions by certain countries in industrial policy are not consistent with the assumptions of "traditional theories on both strategic trade and investment policies, and internationalization motives". Following from that, Buckley (2020) stated that the tensions between the USA and China along with the Covid-19 pandemic are raising VUCA (volatility, uncertainty, complexity, and ambiguity) and therefore both increased antagonism and new forms of cooperation can be expected.

It may still be too soon to fully understand the sources of international competitiveness brought by digitalization. But there is no doubt that the digital economy has had, and is expected to continue having, a big impact on the main pillars of internationalization theories (Banalieva & Dhanaraj, 2019). The extensive use of information technology has modified the internationalization process by reducing transaction costs (Brouthers et al., 2016) and also by increasing network economies, speed, and scalability (Singh & Kundu, 2002). It has also modified the nature of firm-specific advantages and capabilities (Strange & Zucchella, 2017).

The digitalization of the economy has also blurred some of the differences between advanced and emerging markets. Most countries have established good and reliable [internet] networks allowing firms to deploy their business models efficiently (therefore reducing transaction costs), providing scale to strengthen their firm-specific advantages, and also reducing the impact of the local IE (Witt, 2019). Smaller companies and even individuals/freelancers have also benefited from digitalization by reaching customers far away from their home base. And the Covid-19 pandemic has accelerated many behavioral changes in customers and companies that are expected to have a long-lasting impact on the way firms operate across borders (Fornes & Rovira, 2020).

As a consequence, three main challenges are appearing for internationalization theories in the digital economy (Banalieva & Dhanaraj, 2019, pp. 1382–1383). First, the very definition of MNE, one that traditionally has included the investment and deployment of physical assets overseas as a key indicator of internationality. Digital technologies have allowed MNEs to exchange data and tackle markets abroad through digital networks. The idea of place/location moves from physical and territorial attributes to digital, information flow-based features (Kobrin, 2017). Also, the MNE is no longer an isolated unit (the focus of analysis in extant theories), rather it has taken the form of a "digitally networked ecosystem" (DNE). In fact, digital-based multinational corporations are light on physical assets, they use platforms and scale instead to leverage their FSAs with the complementary resources of local partners (Collinson & Narula, 2014).

Second, price-setting has changed. Before digitalization, the preferences of consumers were over-simplified and condensed using data analysis methods constrained by the analog economy. Digitalization has changed the concept of the market "from a common physical space for buyer–seller interactions incentivized by the pricing mechanism to a data-rich environment that buyers and suppliers co-create through new digital technologies". As a consequence, businesses that are strong in the collection and analysis of data have the ability to characterize their customers based on personal preferences, convenience, taste, etc and not only on demand elasticity (Thornhill, 2018). Therefore the pricing of data-rich digital goods is driven more by value-optimization for the users on the network than by marginal cost, as the marginal cost of copying and transferring these types of products globally is almost zero (Schonberger & Ramge, 2018).

Third, as markets are becoming data-rich environments, digitalization is altering the governance of technology and FSAs based on human capital. Digital-based multinational corporations may be able to use their technology FSAs to replace their human capital FSAs (IMF, 2020). This can have an impact on income inequality and unemployment, and therefore affect demand, markets, and as a consequence the internationalization drivers, motives, and strategies.

2.3   Concluding Remarks

This chapter presented a critical overview of mainstream internationalization theories, starting from those developed in the West in the second part of the last century and continuing with those developed for emerging markets-based firms that appeared at the beginning of the 21st century. The focus of this analysis, in the last part of the chapter, has been on the explanatory power of these theories in a highly digitalized environment.

There are several authors who argue that the analytical approach of internationalization theories is still valid; although they were developed in a period where goods and therefore manufacturing abroad were the main drivers to internationalize the operations, in the last 20 years services have also become a major driver to growth internationally (as will be seen in the next chapters). But at the same time these authors recognize that there are some elements that need to be adapted to fully capture the picture. In particular, the following are the main areas where digitalization has had a major impact on the international expansion of companies:

- Reduction of transaction costs,
- Increase of network economies, speed, and scalability (most of them brought by platforms as will be seen in Chap. 4),
- The nature of firm-specific advantages and capabilities,
- The definition of MNEs and the idea of digitally networked ecosystems,
- The place/location moving from physical and territorial attributes, to digital and information flow-based attributes, and
- Price setting.

Following this idea, the next chapter will further study the academic literature and will develop a deeper analysis of each of the elements of mainstream internationalization strategies with a critical focus on their suitability and validity to explain the current international expansion of companies developing their activities in globalized and digitalized environments and experiencing exponential growth. The analysis is intended to shed some light on how digitalization affects the international expansion of firms, especially non-digital born companies.

References

Altamira, M. (2021). *The role of home institutions in the development of marketing capabilities. Competitive advantages at home and abroad in Chinese companies expanding their operations in the European Union.* (PhD). University of Warwick, United Kingdom.

Banalieva, E. R., & Dhanaraj, C. (2019). Internationalization theory for the digital economy. *Journal of International Business Studies, 50*, 1372–1387.

Barney, J. (1991). Firm resources and sustained competitive advantage. *Journal of Management, 17*(1), 99–120.

Barney, J., Wright, M., & Ketchen, D. (2001). The resource-based view of the firm: Ten years after 1991. *Journal of Management, 27*, 625–641.

Boisot, M., & Meyer, M. (2008). Which way through the open door? Reflections on the internationalization of Chinese firms. *Management and Organization Review, 4*(3), 349–365.

Brache, J., & Felzensztein, C. (2019). Exporting firm's engagement with trade associations: Insights from Chile. *International Business Review, 28*, 25–35.

Brouthers, K., Geisser, K., & Rothlauf, F. (2016). Explaining the internationalization of ibusiness firms. *Journal of International Business Studies, 47*(5), 513–534.

Buckley, P. (2018). Internalisation theory and outward direct investment by emerging market multinationals. *Management International Review, 58*, 195–224.

Buckley, P. J. (2020). The theory and empirics of the structural reshaping of globalization. *Journal of International Business Studies, 51*(9), 1580–1592. https://doi.org/10.1057/s41267-020-00355-5

Buckley, P., & Casson, M. (1976). *The future of the multinational enterprise.* Macmillan.

Buckley, P., Clegg, J., Cross, A., Liu, X., Voss, H., & Zheng, P. (2007). The determinants of Chinese outward foreign direct investment. *Journal of International Business Studies, 38*(4), 499–518.

Buckley, P., Clegg, J., Voss, H., Cross, A., Liu, X., & Zheng, P. (2018). A retrospective and agenda for future research on Chinese outward foreign direct investment. *Journal of International Business Studies, 49*, 4–23.

Calhoun, M. (2002). Unpacking liability of foreignness: Identifying culturally driven external and internal sources of liability for the foreign subsidiary. *Journal of International Management, 8*(3), 301–321.

Camison, C., & Villar-Lopez, A. (2010). Effect of SMEs international experience on foreign intensity and economic performance: The mediating role of internationally exploitable assets and competitive strategy. *Journal of Small Business Management, 48*, 116–151.

Cardoza, G., Fornes, G., Farber, V., Gonzalez Duarte, R., & Ruiz Gutierrez, J. (2016). Barriers and public policies affecting the international expansion of Latin American SMEs. Evidence from Brazil, Colombia, and Peru. *Journal of Business Research, 69*(6), 2030–2039.

Casson, M. (2000). *Economics of international business.* Edward Elgar.

Caves, R. (1971). International corporations: The industrial economics of foreign investment. *Economica, 38*, 1.

Caves, R. (1974). Industrial Organization. In J. Dunning (Ed.), *Economic analysis and the multinational Enterprise.* Allen & Unwin.

Cavusgil, S., & Zou, S. (1994). Marketing strategy - performance relationship: An investigation of the empirical link in export market ventures. *Journal of Marketing, 58*, 1–21.

Chen, H., & Chen, T. (1998). Network linkages and location choice in foreign direct investment. *Journal of International Business Studies, 29*(3), 1.

Child, J., & Rodrigues, S. (2005). The internationalization of Chinese firms: A case for theoretical extension? *Management and Organization Review, 1*(3), 381–410.

Collinson, S. C., & Narula, R. (2014). Asset recombination in international partnerships as a source of improved innovation capabilities in China. *The Multinational Business Review, 22*(4), 394–417. https://doi.org/10.1108/MBR-09-2014-0046

Conner, K., & Prahalad, C. (1996). A resource-based theory of the firm: Knowledge versus opportunism. *Organization Science, 7*(5), 477–501.

Cuervo-Cazurra, Á., Maloney, M., & Manrakhan, S. (2007). Causes of the difficulties in internationalization. *Journal of International Business Studies, 38*, 709–725.

Davis, L., & North, D. (1971). *Institutional change and American economic growth*. Cambridge University Press.

Delios, A., & Beamish, P. (2001). Survival and profitability: The roles of experience and intangible assets in foreign subsidiary performance. *Academy of Management Journal, 44*, 1028–1038.

Deng, P. (2011). The internationalization of Chinese firms: a critical review and future research. *International Journal of Management Reviews, DOI:* https://doi.org/10.1111/j.1468-2370.2011.00323.x.

Doz, Y., Asakawa, K., Santos, J., & Williamson, P. (1997). The metanational corporation. *INSEAD working paper.*

Dunning, J. (1977). Trade, location of economic activity, and the MNE: A search for an ecletic approach. In B. Ohlin, P. O. Hesselborn, & P. M. Wijkman (Eds.), *The international allocation of economic activity*. Macmillan.

Dunning, J. (1995). Reappraising the eclectic paradigm in the age of alliance capitalism. *Journal of International Business Studies, 26*, 1.

Dunning, J. (1996). The geographical sources of competitiveness of firms: The results of a new survey. *Transnational Corporations, 5*(3), 1.

Dunning, J. (2001a). The eclectic (OLI) paradigm of international production: Past, present, and future. *Journal of the Economics of Business, 8*(2), 1.

Dunning, J. H. (2001b). *Oxford handbook of international business*. Oxford University Press.

Dunning, J. (2003). Some antecedents of internalization theory. *Journal of International Business Studies, 34*(2), 108–115.

Dunning, J., & Lundan, S. (1998). The geographical sources of competitiveness. *International Business Review, 7*(2), 1.

Enright, M. (1998). Regional clusters and firm strategy. In A. Chandler, P. Hagstrom, & O. Solvell (Eds.), *The dynamic firm*. Oxford University Press.

Enright, M. (2000). The globalization of competition and the localization of competitive advantages: Policies towards regional clustering. In N. Hood & S. Young (Eds.), *The globalization of multinational Enterprise activity*. Macmillan.

Estrin, S., & Prevezer, M. (2011). The role of informal institutions in corporate governance: Brazil, Russia, India, and China compared. *Asia Pacific Journal of Management, 28*(1), 41–67.

Florida, R. (1995). Towards the learning region. *Futures, 27*, 1.

Fornes, G. (2009). *Foreign exchange exposure in emerging markets. How companies can minimize it*. Palgrave Macmillan.

Fornes, G., & Butt Philip, A. (2014). Chinese outward investments to emerging markets. Evidence from Latin America. *European Business Review, 26*(6), 1.

Fornes, G., & Cardoza, G. (2018). Internationalization of Chinese SMEs: The perception of disadvantages of foreignness. *Emerging Markets Finance and Trade*. https://doi.org/10.1080/1540496X.2018.1518218

Fornes, G., & Cardoza, G. (2019). Internationalization of Chinese SMEs: The perception of disadvantages of foreignness. *Emerging Markets Finance and Trade, 55*(9), 2086–2105.

Fornes, G., & Mendez, A. (2018). *The China-Latin America Axis. Emerging markets and their role in an increasingly globalised world*. Palgrave Macmillan.

Fornes, G., & Rovira, J. (2020). Emerging economies and the Covid-19 crisis. In G. L. Gardini (Ed.), *The world before and after Covid-19*. European Institute of International Studies Press.

Fornes, G., Cardoza, G., & Altamira, M. (2021). Do political and business relations help emerging markets' SMEs in their national and international expansion? Evidence from Brazil and China. *International Journal of Emerging Markets*. doi: https://doi.org/10.1108/IJOEM-01-2020-0058

Goel, S., & Karri, R. (2006). Entrepreneurs, Effectual Logic, and Over-Trust *Entrepreneurship Theory and Practice*.

Hennart, J.-F. (2019). Digitalized service multinationals and international business theory. *Journal of International Business Studies, 50*(8), 1388–1400. https://doi.org/10.1057/s41267-019-00256-2

Hofstede, G. (1981). Culture and organizations. *International Studies of Management and Organization, 10*(4), 15–41.

Hoskisson, R. E., Eden, L., Lau, C. M., & Wright, M. (2000). Strategy in emerging economies. *Academy of Management Journal, 43*(3), 249–267.

Hymer, S. (1960). *The international operations of national firms: A study of foreign direct investment*. MIT Press.

Hymer, S. (1968). La grande 'corporation' multinationale: Analyse de certaines raisons qui poussant à l'intégration internationale des affaires. *Reveu Economique, 14*(6), 1.

IMF. (2020). *Global outlook update*. World Bank.

Johanson, J., & Vahlne, J. (1977). The internationalization process of the firm. A model of knowledge development and increasing foreign market commitments. *Journal of International Business Studies, 8*, 23–32.

Johanson, J., & Vahlne, J. (2009). The Upssala internationalization process model revisited: From liability of foreignness to liability of outsidership. *Journal of International Business Studies, 40*(9), 1411–1431.

Karhunen, P., Kosonen, R., McCarthy, D., & Puffer, S. (2018). The darker side of social networks in transforming economies: Corrupt exchange in Chinese guanxi and Russian Blat/Svyazi. *Management and Organization Review, 14*(2), 395–419.

Khanna, T., & Palepu, K. (1997). Why focused strategies may be wrong for emerging markets. *Harvard Business Review, 4*(75), 3–10.

Khanna, T., & Palepu, K. (2000). The future of business groups in emerging markets: Long-run evidence from Chile. *Academy of Management Journal, 43*(3), 268–285.

Khanna, T., & Palepu, K. (2010). *Winning in emerging markets: A road map for strategy and execution*. Harvard Business School Publishing Corporation.

Kittilaksanawong, W. (2017). Institutional distances, resources and entry strategies: Evidence from newly industrialized economy firms. *International Journal of Emerging Markets, 12*(1), 58–78. https://doi.org/10.1108/IJoEM-12-2014-0196

Kobrin, S. J. (2017). Bricks and mortar in a borderless world: Globalization, the backlash, and the multinational Enterprise. *Global Strategy Journal, 7*(2), 159–171. https://doi.org/10.1002/gsj.1158

Kogut, B., & Kulatilaka, N. (1994). Operational flexibility, global manufacturing, and the option value of a multinational network. *Management Science, 40*, 1.

Kogut, B., & Singh, H. (1988). The effect of national culture on the choice of entry mode. *Journal of International Business Studies, 19*(3), 411–432.

Kogut, B., & Zander, I. (1994). Knowledge of the firm and the evolutionary theory of the multinational corporation. *Journal of International Business Studies, 24*(4), 1.

Kojima, K. (1982). Macro economic versus international business approaches to foreign direct investments. *Hotosubashi Journal of Economics, 23*, 1.

Kuemmerle, W. (1999). The drivers of foreign direct investment into research and development: An empirical investment. *Journal of International Business Studies, 30*(1), 1.

Ma, J. (2018). Speech at the World Economic Forum.

Malmberg, A., Solvell, O., & Zander, I. (1996). Spatial clustering, local accumulation of knowledge and firm competitiveness. *Geographical Annals, 78*(2), 1.

Mathews, J. (2006). Dragon multinationals: New players in 21st century globalization. *Asia Pacific Journal of Management, 23*(1), 5–27.

Mathews, J. (2018). Dragon multinationals powered by linkage, leverage and learning: A review and development. *Asia Pacific Journal of Management, 34*, 769–775.

McManus, J. (1972). The theory of the international firm. In G. Paquet (Ed.), *The multinational firm and the nation state.* Collins and Macmillan.

Moon, H. (1999). *An unconventional theory of foreign direct investment.* Seoul National University.

Narula, R., Asmussen, C. G., Chi, T., & Kundu, S. K. (2019). Applying and advancing internalization theory: The multinational enterprise in the twenty-first century. *Journal of International Business Studies, 50*(8), 1231–1252. https://doi.org/10.1057/s41267-019-00260-6

North, D. (1984). Transaction costs, institutions, and economic history. *Journal of Institutional and Theoretical Economics, 140*, 7–17.

North, D. (1990). *Institutions, institutional change, and economic performance.* Cambridge University Press.

North, D. (1991). Institutions. *The Journal of Economic Perspectives, 5*(1), 97–112.

North, D. (1993). The new institutional economics and development. Retrieved from Http://econwpa.wustl.edu:8089/eps/eh/papers/9309/9309001.pdf

North, D. (1995). Five propositions about institutional change. In J. Knight & I. Sened (Eds.), *Exploring social institutions.* University of Michigan Press.

North, D. (2005). *Understanding the process of economic change.* Princeton University Press.

Park, S., & Luo, Y. (2001). Guanxi and organizational dynamics: Organizational networking in Chinese firms. *Strategic Management Journal, 22*(5), 455–477.

Peng, M., Lee, S.-H., & Wang, D. (2005). What determines the scope of the firm over time? A focus on institutional relatedness. *Academy of Management Review, 30*(3), 622–633.

Peng, M., Wang, D., & Jiang, Y. (2008). An institution-based view of international business strategy: A focus on emerging economies. *Journal of International Business Studies, 39*, 920–936.

Penrose, E. (1959). *The theory of the growth of the firm.* Sharpe.

Petricevic, O., & Teece, D. J. (2019). The structural reshaping of globalization: Implications for strategic sectors, profiting from innovation, and the multinational enterprise. *Journal of International Business Studies, 50*(9), 1487–1512. https://doi.org/10.1057/s41267-019-00269-x

Pollman, E., & Barry, J. (2017). Regulatory entrepreneurship. *Southern California Law Review, 90*, 383–448.

Rauch, J., & Trindade, V. (2002). Ethnic Chinese networks in international trade. *The Review of Economics and Statistics, February, 1*, 116–130.

Ruan, J. (2017). *Guanxi, social capital and school choice in China. The rise of ritual capital.* Palgrave Macmillan.

Rugman, A., & Li, J. (2007). Will China's multinationals succeed globally or regionally? *European Management Journal, 25*(5), 333–343.

Schonberger, V., & Ramge, T. (2018). *Reinventing capitalism in the age of big data.* Basic Books.

Shi, W., Sun, L., Yan, D., & Zhu, Z. (2017). Institutional fragility and outward foreign direct investment from China. *Journal of International Business Studies, 48*, 452–476.

Singh, N., & Kundu, S. (2002). Explaining the growth of E-commerce corporations (ECCs): An extension and application of the eclectic paradigm. *Journal of International Business Studies, 33*(4), 679–697. https://doi.org/10.1057/palgrave.jibs.8491039

Solvell, O., & Birkinshaw, J. (2000). Multinational enterprises and the knowledge economy: Leveraging global practices. In J. Dunning (Ed.), *Regions, globalisation, and the knowledge based economy.* Oxford University Press.

Storper, M., & Scott, H. (1995). The wealth of regions. *Futures, 27*(5), 1.

Strange, R., & Zucchella, A. (2017). Industry 4.0, global value chains and international business. *Multinational Business Review, 25*(3), 174–184. https://doi.org/10.1108/MBR-05-2017-0028

Suseno, Y., & Pinnington, A. (2018). Building social capital and human capital for internationalization: The role of network ties and knowledge resources. *Asia Pacific Journal of Management, 35*, 1081–1106.

Thornhill, J. (2018, April 2, 2018). The rise of the information economy threatens traditional companies. *Financial Times.* Retrieved from https://www.ft.com/content/6c6c730e-3298-11e8-ac48-10c6fdc22f03

UNCTAD. (2022). Global foreign direct investment flows over the last 30 years. Retrieved from https://unctad.org/data-visualization/global-foreign-direct-investment-flows-over-last-30-years

Vassolo, R., De Castro, J., & Gomez-Mejia, L. (2011). Managing in Latin America: Common issues and a research agenda. *Academy of Management Perspectives, 1*, 22–36.

Vernon, R. (1966). International investment and international trade in the product cycle. *Quarterly Journal of Economics, 80*(2), 190. Retrieved from http://search.epnet.com/login.aspx?direct=true&db=buh&an=4966727

Vernon, R. (1974). The location of economic activity. In J. Dunning (Ed.), *Economic analysis and the multinational Enterprise*. Allen & Unwin.

Wesson, T. (1993). *An alternative motivation for foreign direct investment*. Harvard University Press.

Wesson, T. (1997). *A model of asset seeking foreign direct investment*. Paper presented at the The Administration Science Association of Canada.

Williamson, O. (1985). *The economic institutions of capitalism: Firms, markets, relational contracting*. Free Press.

Witt, M. A. (2019). De-globalization: Theories, predictions, and opportunities for international business research. *Journal of International Business Studies, 50*(7), 1053–1077. https://doi.org/10.1057/s41267-019-00219-7

Wright, M., Filatotchev, I., Hoskisson, R. E., & Peng, M. W. (2005). Strategy research in emerging economies: Challenging the conventional wisdom. *Journal of Management Studies, 42*(1), 1–33.

Zaheer, S. (1995). Overcoming the liability of foreignness. *Academy of Management Journal, 38*(2), 341–363.

Zeng, M., & Williamson, J. (2003). The hidden dragons *Harvard Business Review, October 2003*, 92–99.

Zheng, N., & Qu, Y. (2015). What explains the performance of Chinese exporting firms? *Journal of Chinese Economic and Business Studies, 13*(1), 51–70.

Zhou, L. (2007). The effects of entrepreneurial proclivity and foreign market knowledge on early internationalization. *Journal of World Business, 42*, 281–293.

3

Internationalization, Digitalization, and Exponential Growth

Abstract Building on the previous section, chapter 3 critically analyzes the three most relevant internationalization theories (Uppsala model, OLI and LLL) and assesses whether they can still explain the international expansion of firms in the new digital era. It also discusses how digitalization affects the international expansion of non-digital-born firms. Digitalization and international expansion are still an emerging area of research but it seems evident from the analysis that there are opportunities for more explicit theoretical links between digitalization and international expansion. The discussion section in the chapter shows that the adoption of digital technologies positively impacts the internationalization process of firms. Digital technologies facilitate the development of internationalization strategies, contributing to firms' accelerated and/or exponential growth. Consequently, it seems that mainstream theories are still valid to explain the international expansion of companies in an increasing digitalized environment, but that some adaptations and new variables are needed to fully explain the impact of digitalization. Examples and cases are presented with a focus on international trade of services and its exponential growth in the past decade, and how this phenomenon may impact internationalization theories.

Keywords Uppsala Model • OLI • LLL • Non-digital firms •
Digitalization • Exponential growth • Liability of foreignness

> *"Around 400 million people in the last year [2014] got a smartphone. If you
> think that's a big deal, imagine the impact on that person in the
> developing world."*
> —Eric Schmidt, Executive Chairman, Google, USA *(Schmidt, 2015)*

3.1   Introduction

International expansion is a strategic decision and a relevant source of
companies' growth and sustained competitive advantage. Recent research
on international business and strategy shows there is a growing interest in
understanding the link between digitalization and internationalization
and the impact of new digital technologies on the internationalization
process. The increasing use of these technologies, the adoption of digital
services and further digital transformation processes are shaping not only
the internationalization pathway of companies but why and how they
decide to go abroad too; and more importantly, how companies can grow
(eventually at higher rates).

A recent literature review about digitalization and international expansion confirmed the relevance and the positive influence of the adoption
of digital services and new digital technologies on the international
expansion of firms (Ojala et al., 2022). Digitalization makes markets
naturally global, improves the accessibility to products and services globally, and enhances new ways of entering international markets. With new
digital technologies in the value chain, firms are in a better position to (i)
find new opportunities in more innovative ways, and (ii) target more
potential consumers (Hervé et al., 2020). However, research seems to be
in its early stages. The literature shows that most of the studies developed
in the area to date have taken digitalization for granted, meaning that

there is still an opportunity for a deeper understanding of how and why the adoption of digital services, digital activities, or new technologies enhances and promotes the benefits of the international expansion of the firm.

It is in this context where there is the need to develop a more robust theoretical approach to further analyze and understand the impact of digitalization on existing and new internationalization theories that better explain the international expansion of firms in the context of increasing digitalization. Moreover, most of the research developed to date is based on service providers, digital platforms providers, or digital devices providers, meaning that there is an opportunity to further analyze the impact of digitalization on the international expansion of non-digital-born firms. Finally, most of the available studies focus on Western-based companies and apply Western-developed theories (i.e mainly Uppsala and OLI), meaning that there is an interesting opportunity to develop further research on the opportunities that digitalization is bringing to emerging and developing markets and how this affects firms' international expansion.

In sum, a clearer theoretical link between digitalization and international expansion is needed to explain why and how digitalization influences the international expansion of firms (Hervé et al., 2020). While some research on digitalization and international expansion applying the Uppsala model to new-born digitals from developed markets has been developed, further research and a critical analysis of the applicability of other mainstream theories (mainly OLI and LLL) is needed. Therefore, by critically analyzing each of the models, the present chapter attempts to answer the following questions: Can established internationalization theories explain the international expansion of firms operating in the new digital era? How does digitalization affect the international expansion of non-digital-born firms? The chapter will also highlight some areas for future research and will provide a discussion and application of the findings.

3.2   Digitalization and the Uppsala Model

The Uppsala Model has been one of the most discussed internationalization theories and it is widely employed to understand the international expansion of companies. Swedish researchers Johanson and Vahlne (1977) developed the model to explain the four different stages to enter an international market through an increasingly foreign dedication: (i) sporadic exports, (ii) export via a representative in the foreign country, (iii) establishment of a sales subsidiary, and (iv) manufacturing and direct distribution through a foreign subsidiary in the host country. The rationale is that companies expand first to physically and culturally close markets, and only once they have developed sufficient knowledge and improve the acquisition and use of resources do they expand to more distant markets. Close and distant are measured in terms of culture, politics, language, access to information and other resources. It is in this sense that the model links market knowledge, commitment in the market (an increased market knowledge usually leads to a higher commitment), and the results of the initial and subsequent activities in the previous stages as determinants to continue the following phase of internationalization.

In recent years the authors have been updating the model to incorporate the new realities of an increasingly digitalized and globalized environment to the characteristics of the multinational enterprise (MNE). In their view, the foundations (the four stages) of the model remain the same, only several elements that define the evolution towards the MNE (if compared to the definition of the firm in the original version of the theory) are to be considered: processes at different levels, "network rather than a stand-alone unit; business exchange rather than production; proactive and entrepreneurial rather than passive; heterarchical (decentralized) rather than hierarchical" (Coviello et al., 2017, p. 1152). Interestingly, although the authors recognize the relevance of technology in international business, they do not include the concept as an element influencing the internationalization pathway of a firm.

Indeed, this is today the most common criticism of the model along with its limitations to explain the rise of EMs MNEs (Oliveira et al., 2018), its application to EMs being rare (Meyer & Peng, 2016). New digital technologies, and especially the Internet, are providing opportunities to companies that did not exist when the model was developed but are playing a decisive role's in today's increasingly globalized and digitalized world. This means that the model may still be valid in the context of more traditional industries but needs to be rethought or adapted to environments where digital technology is advancing (Arvidsson & Arvidsson, 2019). As previously explained, the four stages of the model have been defined and applied in developed markets but the business and institutional environments in EMs are known to be very different (Rottig, 2016), especially in terms of the access to relevant information, knowledge, and supporting resources (Fornes & Cardoza, 2019).

The access to knowledge about a market and the ability to obtain data of consumers and directly interact with them without being present is now possible thanks to digital technologies. With this information firms can improve the understanding of consumers' needs and therefore adapt their offer reducing thus the psychological and cultural distance. This means that companies no longer depend on engaging first with culturally closed environments. On the contrary, technology opens a full range of opportunities to target varied markets (even simultaneously), not necessarily culturally close, facilitating the access to resources and the development of capabilities. This challenges the link between market knowledge, commitment in the market, and the results of the initial stages to move to the next one.

Furthermore, with the use of digital technologies, communication, distribution, and production channels are dematerialized and as a consequence markets become instantaneous, with no geographical distances or borders where companies and customers can meet directly (Hervé et al., 2020). The Internet and digital platforms provide the opportunity to instantly sell to markets far from the home market, offering firms the possibility of exponential growth, engaging in a foreign market without the need of going through the different stages stated by the Uppsala model. In addition, the reliance on networks to grow and expand questions the liability of foreignness. Digital technologies allow firms to overcome this liability through the creation and coordination of a network of users and collaborators, the sharing of data, and the development and use of digital platforms (Hervé et al., 2020).

All in all, technology and the use of digital technologies impact the way firms expand abroad, the type of market companies target, and the speed of companies entering new markets. They also challenge the [theoretical] steps to engage with foreign markets and therefore the internationalization process. Digitalization also increases the speed and agility at which firms can create and expand their networks, and considering the democratization of global consumption and the improvement of communication and information exchange, there is no clear need to grow and expand in stages (Coviello et al., 2017).

3.3   Digitalization and OLI

The OLI framework/Eclectic Paradigm, as seen in the previous chapter, helps firms to determine to what extent it is beneficial to pursue FDI or alternatively engage with a different/more suitable approach to international production such as exports, licenses, franchises, or strategic alliances. Despite the fact that the framework was devised around forty years ago (and therefore in a completely different business environment), it has been widely used and adapted to the evolution of globalization. The framework is based on the assumption that firms invest in international markets to acquire/get access to resources that are available at lower costs overseas, therefore companies engage in foreign production mainly to take advantage of low costs abroad, using their own assets (advantages) while internalizing costs. Thus, it seems that the bases of the theory might need to be reshaped by digitalization and digital globalization (Luo, 2021).

Following the rationale of the OLI framework, in order to engage in international production, a company first needs an Ownership Advantage that leads to a sustained competitive advantage over foreign competitors in the host market. Examples of competitive advantage capabilities can be a strong brand, copyrights, technological superiority, or a sound reputation. In this context, Dunning (2015) distinguished among these advantages/capabilities (i) the assets linked to proprietary ownership, and (ii) the transaction advantages that lead to efficient internal transaction costs.

Digitalization has reshaped the business environment in which multinational enterprises operate, and therefore the sources of competitive advantage both at home and in foreign markets have changed. In the current complex and dynamic markets, companies need to possess key assets and capabilities to succeed against fierce competition, and also need to have the ability to develop dynamic and adaptive capabilities (Fornes et al., 2021; Luo, 2021; Teece et al., 1997). Dynamic capabilities are augmented, reconfigured, or newly developed capabilities intended to look for new opportunities in changing and dynamic environments. Adaptive capabilities are based on flexible processes that can be reconfigured and redefined according to changes in the market and therefore enable anticipation. These capabilities are extremely relevant for companies operating in different markets; in the current digital and globalized environment there is efficient access to resources from different places worldwide, which means that firms need to anticipate changes, look for new opportunities, be flexible, and eventually can compete without the need of possessing unique assets or market power.

Digital technologies have a major impact on distance and location as well. As previously mentioned, physical borders have become almost non-relevant and at the same time operations can be internationalized relatively quickly. In this context, a multinational organization can manage international activities online, reducing thus the psychological distance, and international activities and production can be supported by business networks, reducing thus transaction costs. This means that through the use of digital technologies firms can make strategic decisions focusing on proximity to the target market and customers rather than [only] on production costs as suggested by OLI (Strange & Zucchella, 2017).

Indeed, in the current global value chains, digital technologies make innovation and speed more important than production costs and distance (Cavusgil & Knight, 2015; Foss, 2005). The focus is no longer on where to manufacture, but rather on meeting strategic interests, or on a location that can best support the entire company's value chain. In fact, Cano-Kollmann, Cantwell, Hannigan, Mudambi, and Song (2016) argued that International Business research should evolve from "location analysis" to "spatial analysis" where space includes geographic locations as well as social, technological, or institutional. Digitalization connects people, organizations, and places in a virtual environment, questioning therefore the "location" advantage of the OLI framework.

Finally, the Eclectic Paradigm relies on the assumption that companies internalize foreign markets when the benefits of doing so exceed the internal costs. However, there is a global intermediary market that offers multiple options to companies for their international expansion strategy, so their decisions do not depend only on the original rationale. In fact, the access to global markets has improved the availability of value added inputs, such as technology, digital distribution, marketing and branding, etc. Emerging technologies, such as artificial intelligence, can also be applied to improve production and distribution in host markets (Kraus et al., 2019; Aagaard et al., 2019; Watson et al., 2018). In this context, as external resources have become widely available and easily accessible, companies are increasingly leveraging on the value of external networks to cope with an increasing global competition. This means that multinationals are much more active in looking for these networks to enhance their internalization advantages. Also, through the use of the Internet and platforms, the potential benefit of internalizing some costs (such as research or knowledge costs) are being reduced almost every day (Luo, 2021).

In conclusion, digitalization and technology are shaping the motivations and pillars on which companies based their international expansion, and therefore challenge the concept of the 'advantages' in the OLI framework. This is particularly evident in environments or industries in which technology is of key importance in the [global] value chain. Some authors have proposed new complementary advantages to adapt the framework to the new digitalized and globalized environment, including digitally enabled global open resource access, digitally enabled connectivity-based linkage, and digitally enabled integration advantages (Luo, 2021). The OLI framework is still valid, their original 'advantages' are of less importance, but it is strengthened by new advantages underpinned by technology. The applicability of these new advantages and how they complement with the original ones need to be further analyzed and tested. More specifically, new research on specific industries and sectors as well as on different types of firms, beyond giant technological companies, born-digital firms and technological start-ups is needed. Digitalization provides a full range of opportunities in a globalized environment, especially boosting international exponential growth; all types of firms engaging with technology, regardless of their level of digitalization, can seize these opportunities.

3.4 Digitalization and LLL

The understanding of the internationalization pathway of companies from emerging markets has been gaining increasing interest among international business scholars in the past decades, especially since the rise of Chinese multinationals. While most scholars had been applying the frameworks seen in the first part of this chapter to analyze the behavior of the companies, Mathews (2006) was one of the first authors to challenge the application of theories developed for/with Western companies to study EM-based enterprises. In the analysis of what were called Dragon Multinationals, the author explained that firms from EMs experience business environments with different institutional frameworks than the ones found in Western markets. These companies were characterized by weak substantial prior resources in their home markets along with other distinctive characteristics compared to incumbent firms, namely (i) accelerated internationalization, (ii) organizational innovation, and (iii) strategic innovation, emphasizing the idea that traditional theories do not necessarily apply. It was in this context that he developed the linkage, leverage, and learning (LLL) strategy as a way of accounting for these characteristics and the highly distinctive strategies followed by latecomer firms from EMs.

According to Mathews, the internationalization of EMs firms starts with resources acquired externally in international markets (Linkage) rather than taken from their own advantages and capabilities (as is the case with Western companies). This is because companies from EMs lack superior competitive advantages or possess capabilities that may not be transferable to international markets (He et al., 2019; Peng et al., 2018). Leverage, therefore, refers to the EM multinationals' ability to take advantage of these capabilities within their international network, basically leveraging (so to speak) on someone else's capabilities. EM-based

firms have demonstrated an efficient establishment of structures and processes that enable them to effectively manage and utilize the resources
and capabilities across the entire network. Finally, it is the subsequent
Learning processes that accelerate expansion patterns; companies apply
repeated linkage and leverage processes that lead to organizational learning processes.

In his 2017 review, Mathews (2017) recognized that there have been
astonishing changes in the international business system and that the
LLL strategizing is indeed adapted to the "interconnected, interlinked
character of the global economy into which new dragon multinationals
are expanding" (p. 772). The author emphasized that the fundamentals
of the LLL as a strategic framework remain, although adaptations such as
the need to differentiate between the capabilities acquired through linkage and learning and the development of unique and new capabilities
that some firms have demonstrated to outcompete global leaders is
needed. However, the role of digitalization and the impact of new digital
technologies have not yet been included in the analysis, opening opportunities for further research in the area, especially when it is evident that
the adoption of digital technologies can have an impact in enhancing and
facilitating the development of links across borders or promoting faster
learning processes.

Indeed, the need for this research becomes even more relevant due to
the recent accelerating digitalization in EMs, a phenomenon explaining
the rapid development of these markets, especially in Asia. The fast speed
of change and disruption happening in emerging countries, enhanced by
specific policies and investments in quality digital infrastructures, is
expected to help to address poverty and inequalities while fostering
growth and the recovery from Covid-19 (Asian Development Bank,
2022; Fornes & Rovira, 2020). In addition, digitalization via capital
input has a positive social and environmental impact while at the same
time enhancing efficiency, inclusiveness, and promoting innovation.
Other benefits include a more efficient energy use, easier financial access
for unserved markets or better inclusiveness. In this sense digitalization
and the adoption of new technologies positively contribute to sustainable
growth and have an impact on how firms develop their businesses and on
the development of new capabilities.

From an internationalization perspective, the impact of digitalization on firms' business development is in line with Mathews' reflection on the need for new in-house unique technology management-related capabilities for EMs' firms to compete with global players. Within this, and deepening the understanding of the LLL framework, digitalization facilitates and speeds the processes of identifying, developing, and implementing the necessary international connections and partnerships, enabling thus access to resources and complementary assets. Also, digitalization, the adoption of new technologies, and the subsequent development of digital skills, boost the capacity of developing high-end expertise with international partners, focusing more easily on R&D international networks, enhancing and encouraging innovation as a consequence.

In addition to establishing and developing an international network, EMs-based firms need to leverage these linkages. For this, companies create structures to manage and deploy, efficiently, the capabilities throughout the entire network. EMs' multinationals have usually leveraged resources through knowledge sharing. Through the use of digital technologies, such as cloud computing or data analytics, firms enhance and facilitate knowledge sharing while making processes more efficient, helping, therefore to leverage the acquired competences. The increasing engagement with digital technologies has been affecting positively the internationalization strategies and efforts of these companies, similar to what has been happening in Western markets.

Weaknesses for EMs-based companies are still tangible regardless of the increasing digitalization. This is due to information problems usually existing in EMs and the poor and not always available comprehensive, reliable, and objective information to make decisions, or the misguided regulations and the prioritization of political goals over economic efficiency (Cardoza et al., 2015; Hoskisson et al., 2000; Ramamurti, 2012; Rottig, 2016). These information-related weaknesses limit the potential benefits of digitalization. For example, the development of better interconnected networks leading to fewer social, economic, and cultural barriers can help to take full advantage of the business opportunities offered by the adoption of digital technologies, not only in the domestic context but internationally too.

Having said this, only a few EMs have fully engaged with digitalization (Asian Development Bank, 2022). This means that it may be too soon to fully understand the impact of digitalization on the internationalization process of firms from EMs as well as on the institutional and business environment in these markets. There are also very few publications and little research developed to date focused on analyzing the impact and effects of digitalization in emerging countries. In this context, from a theoretical perspective, further studies on how the LLL strategic framework is being impacted by digitalization should be developed; in other words, whether and how digitalization is shaping the internationalization expansion of companies from EMs while analyzing whether a new approach to understand more recent international expansion processes may be needed.

3.5   Discussion and Application

Digitalization and globalization have been growing increasingly intertwined as seen in Chapter 1, especially from the late 90s and early 2000s. Many countries opened their economies to international trade and foreign investments, and at the same time information and communication technologies helped the world to be closer. On the one hand, opening the economies helped to decouple the firm from the factor endowment of a single nation and made raw materials, components, machinery, and other services available globally on comparable terms (Porter, 1998). On the other hand, ICT reduced the time and cost of travel, lowered the cost of exchanging factors (or factor dependent goods) among markets, and brought rapid exchanges of information (Brakman et al., 2006; McDonald & Burton, 2002). The main consequence of this was that companies got access to new and diverse markets within shorter timeframes, with relatively lower investments, and with more efficient control tools.

There is an example from the late 90s of a manufacturing SME based in the West of Argentina. They wanted to sell to Chile, so for this they drove around 350km crossing the Andes, and once they arrived in Santiago (the capital city) went to a payphone booth, got the relevant two pages from the Yellow Pages [1], and started visiting potential customers. This two-day trip was less costly than making international calls (very expensive at that time), but more importantly a directory of potential clients was not available. This was only 25 years ago; it is difficult to find these types of difficulties, challenges, costs, and barriers to trade in the world today. The relatively easier access to new markets offers the opportunity for high growth (or exponential growth as it is also called). Probably one of the best examples of this exponential growth have been firms based in China, from operating in a closed economy at the end of the 20th century to achieve leading market share positions in goods by 2020 as can be seen in Fig. 3.1.

During this period, especially in the 90s and early 2000s, many countries embarked on domestic reforms that led them to become increasingly engaged in world trade and investments. These countries are the so-called emerging economies, countries where their governments' policies aimed at economic liberalization and the adoption of a free-market system (Hoskisson et al., 2000). Also, during this period, due to the reforms and the fact that information on the domestic market was not always available, the Location advantage of OLI was a key variable to consider for an international expansion strategy. The World Bank, for example, started to publish the 'Doing Business Report' [2] in 2004 as a way to reduce the information gap. But after a few years, mainly by the end of the 2000s, most of these countries had accessed the WTO and adopted its principles, and also completed the reforms that allowed them to participate in the international trade system. Companies from Mexico, Brazil, Turkey, Chile, Colombia, Eastern European countries, Vietnam, South Africa, India, to name only a few, have benefited from this process. Only a few countries were not fully participating in this system, namely Venezuela, Cuba, and a few more exceptions. In this context, the Location advantage focused decisions on costs (low cost production), access to markets (to

---

[1] For the young readers, the yellow pages were telephone directories of businesses, first published in 1886, organized by category rather than alphabetically by business name, in which advertising was sold. The directories were originally printed on yellow paper, as opposed to white pages for non-commercial listings. The final issue was published in 2019 in the UK.

[2] https://archive.doingbusiness.org/en/doingbusiness

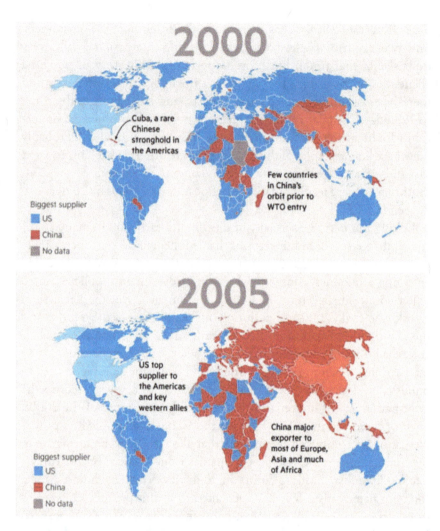

Fig. 3.1 Exponential growth of market share achieved by Chinese companies since 2000. (Adapted from Colback, 2020)

support the growth), and/or access to resources (in particular, technology and talent).

In the early 2020s, the Location advantage is changing its focus again. First due to the disruptions brought by the Covid-19 pandemic and second by what is known as the big decoupling of the world's economy (that

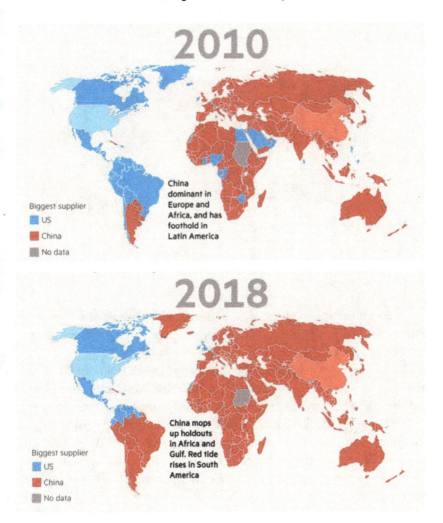

Fig. 3.1 (continued)

is creating two trade and political blocks), Western companies are being encouraged by their governments to shift manufacturing and sourcing components and raw materials to countries with shared values to minimize risks of protectionism, nationalization, uncertainty in the supply chains, etc. This movement was coined "friendshoring" by the US Treasury Secretary Janet Yellen (Wolf, 2022). The Location advantage is

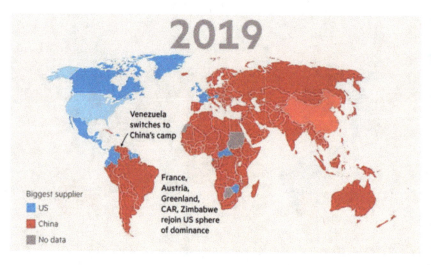

Fig. 3.1 (continued)

also focusing now on minimizing political risk in the host country, or minimizing risks of being caught up in a supply chain or trade dispute between governments.

The liability of foreignness has also changed since it appeared in the late 70s (Johanson & Vahlne, 1977) when most economies were closed and there was little market information [easily] available. Since then the European Single Market [3] came to life creating one of the world's largest consumer markets, new and diverse free trade agreements were signed, English has become the lingua franca in business, or business education has become a global industry where the management of different cultures and environments has been a key field of study (Fornes et al., 2019). In addition, relatively easy access to information about markets from different angles and reputable sources, the possibility of having simultaneous technology-based translation in conversations, the opportunity of having very frequent video calls at a very low cost, etc. are examples of how the digitalization of the economy along with the ubiquitous access to information have reshaped this liability. The current main challenges in terms of liability of foreignness are no longer related to trade barriers (formal

---

[3] https://single-market-economy.ec.europa.eu/single-market_en

and/or informal), cultural differences, language, regulations, or information, they are more associated with the development of relationships and participation in ecosystems like engaging with local networks, understanding the local informal institutions, and identifying the sources of competitiveness in the host market (Altamira et al., 2022; Fornes et al., 2021).

The major beneficiaries of this increase in digitalization and globalization, and as a consequence exponential growth, have been services. The volume of services traded internationally in the late 80s was not significant in comparison with the volume of traded goods, but in 2021 services account for almost 50% of the trade in goods (WTO, 2022). A good example of the opportunities for exponential growth of services, especially one from non-traditional origins, is "BZRP Music Sessions, Vol. 52" [4] (also known as 'Quédate'), a song launched in June 2022 by producer Bizarrap (from Buenos Aires, Argentina) and singer Quevedo (from the Canary Islands, Spain) which within half an hour of its release got one million views on YouTube and 63 million on Spotify (Gonzalez, 2022). The song then reached number one on Spotify Global Top 50 on 16th July 2022 (after around 25 days) and stayed in the top position for more than 30 days, the only song in Spanish to have achieved this; see Fig. 3.2. It also reached number one on Billboard's Global 200 and it was number one in eight different countries (Trust, 2022). Before this hit, Bizarrap was known mainly in Argentina and Quevedo was hardly known in Spain, but they managed to avoid legacy structures in the industry, overcome traditional barriers, and get direct access to the consumer through digital channels.

Education is another good example of a service that in the last decade has crossed the physical boundaries of the classroom, campus, and country to reach a much wider, diverse, and larger audience. For example, from 2011 to 2021 the number of learners reached by massive open online courses (MOOCs) increased exponentially from 300,000 to 220 million (Díaz-Infante et al., 2022). The technology, pedagogic methods, and knowledge have been available for some time, but the restrictions imposed by the Covid-19 pandemic effected a change in the behavior of

---

[4] https://www.youtube.com/watch?v=A_g3lMcWVy0

Fig. 3.2 Tweet from Bizarrap celebrating reaching #1 on Spotify

consumers and accelerated the adoption of online/hybrid education. In fact, between 2012 and 2019 students enrolled in hybrid and distance-only courses increased by 36 percent; between 2020 and 2021 that growth was 92% (Díaz-Infante et al., 2022). Education was one of the few industries resisting the disruption brought by technology but the pandemic weakened this resistance; part of this resistance has been to protect business models based on capital-intensive assets (buildings, accommodation for students, classrooms, etc).

The opening of the world markets to flows of goods and services along with the development of communication and learning technologies are challenging the whole ecosystem and value chain of education. It was only 30 years ago when having access to a deep [on-campus] library was a major source of strength of many education institutions, the same for access to well-equipped laboratories, large lecture theatres, or student dorms. Nowadays, knowledge flows through the internet and is available almost everywhere: 3D printing, virtual and augmented reality along with metaverse-related technologies (what is known as immersive learning) have increased the options for experiential learning and at the same time have drastically reduced the cost of experimenting. Technology also offers alternatives not easily available in the bricks and mortar ecosystem, like the possibility of learning sharing in real time (for example, two surgeons based in different places carrying out a surgery together) or an almost seamless interaction between people speaking different languages. This, as a consequence, has spread the knowledge that before was concentrated in a few areas (mainly the Northeast and West of the US, Northern Europe, and Japan) and also brought access to education to people in places where it was not previously available.

3.6   Concluding Remarks

As can be seen from the analysis presented in this chapter, digitalization and international expansion are still an emerging area of research. In particular, there are opportunities for more explicit theoretical links between digitalization and international expansion, with a focus on the impact of digitalization on internationalization theories. From the discussion developed above, it can be concluded that the adoption of digital technologies positively impacts the internationalization process of firms. Digital technologies facilitate the development of internationalization strategies, contributing to firms' accelerated and/or exponential growth. The analysis has also shown that mainstream theories are still valid to explain the international expansion of companies in an increasing digitalized environment, but it seems clear that some adaptations and new variables are needed to fully explain the impact of digitalization.

This was supported by the examples and cases presented in the discussion section (3.5) which shows how globalization and digitalization have been growing increasingly intertwined. In this context, the Chinese companies that went from small firms to leaders in several world markets in the last 20 years are a case in point. During this period, the analysis of the host markets, and within this the role of the Location advantage, has moved from understanding how these markets work (to leverage the ownership advantage and also to minimize risks) to avoiding being caught in geopolitical disputes (a strategy called "friendshoring" by the US Treasury Secretary). The liability of foreignness has also been reshaped by globalization and digitalization, the world became closer in the last 40 years and therefore the sources of this liability have changed. Currently the liability of foreignness deals with development of relationships, participation in ecosystems, understanding informal institutions, and identifying the sources of competitiveness in host markets.

International trade of services was not significant when the mainstream theories were developed, but now they represent around 50% of the trade in goods. This shows how services have been a major beneficiary of globalization and digitalization; their exponential growth has been supported by an almost direct and seamless access to the final consumer through the internet, facilitated by the widespread reach and low costs of communication technologies. Two examples were used: first, in music, a producer from Argentina working with a singer from the Spanish Canary Island reaching the top of the world market, displacing incumbent players; second, in education, online courses have grown from 300,000 to 220 million in the 10 years before 2021. The growth and reach of education are even more important as it has offered the opportunity to make good/international education available to people that only a few years ago did not have access to education at all.

References

Altamira, M., Fornes, G., & Mendez, A. (2022). Chinese institutions and international expansion within the Belt and Road Initiative: firm capabilities of Chinese companies in the European Union. *Asia Pacific Business Review*. doi: https://doi.org/10.1080/13602381.2022.2093520

Arvidsson, H. G. S., & Arvidsson, R. (2019). The Uppsala model of internationalisation and beyond. *International Journal of Finance and Administration, 42*(2), 221–239.

Asian Development Bank. (2022). *Promoting Digitalization for Green and Inclusive Growth in Asia.* Retrieved from Regional (INO, KOR, MAL, PHI, PRC, SIN, THA, VIE).

Brakman, S., Garretsen, H., van Marrewijk, C., & van Witteloostuijn, A. (2006). *Nations and firms in the global economy. An introduction to international economics and business.* Cambridge University Press.

Cardoza, G., Fornes, G., Li, P., Xu, N., & Xu, S. (2015). China goes global: Public policies' influence on small- and medium-sized enterprises' international expansion. *Asia Pacific Business Review, 21*(2), 188–210.

Coviello, N., Liena, K., & Liesch, P. (2017). Adapting the Uppsala model to a modern world: Macro-context and microfoundations. *Journal of International Business Studies, 48*, 1151–1164.

Díaz-Infante, N., Lazar, M., Ram, S., & Ray, A. (2022, 20 July 2022). Demand for online education is growing. Are providers ready? *McKinsey & Company.* Retrieved from https://www.mckinsey.com/industries/education/our-insights/demand-for-online-education-is-growing-are-providers-ready

Dunning, J. H. (2015). *The eclectic paradigm of international production: A restatement and some possible extensions.* Palgrave Macmillan.

Fornes, G., & Cardoza, G. (2019). Internationalization of Chinese SMEs: The perception of disadvantages of foreignness. *Emerging Markets Finance and Trade, 55*(9), 2086–2105.

Fornes, G., & Rovira, J. (2020). Emerging economies and the Covid-19 crisis. In G. L. Gardini (Ed.), *The world before and after Covid-19.* European Institute of International Studies Press.

Fornes, G., Monfort, A., Ilie, C., Koo, C. K., & Cardoza, G. (2019). Ethics, responsibility, and sustainability in MBAs. Understanding the motivations for the incorporation of ERS in less traditional markets. *Sustainability, 11*, 1.

Fornes, G., Cardoza, G., & Altamira, M. (2021). Do political and business relations help emerging markets' SMEs in their national and international expansion? Evidence from Brazil and China. *International Journal of Emerging Markets.* doi: https://doi.org/10.1108/IJOEM-01-2020-0058

Gonzalez, C. (2022). Bizarrap and Quevedo Achieve the #1 Song on Spotify's Global Top. Retrieved from https://www.jefebet.com/en/featured/bizarrap-and-quevedo-achieve-the-1-song-on-spotifys-global-top/

He, S., Khan, Z., Lew, Y., & Fallon, G. (2019). Technological innovation as a source of Chinese multinationals' firm-specific advantages and internationalization. *International Journal of Emerging Markets, 14*(4), 1. https://doi.org/10.1108/IJOEM-02-2017-0059

Hervé, A., Schmitt, C., & Baldegger, R. (2020). Internationalization and digitalization: Applying digital technologies to the internationalization process of small and medium-sized enterprises. *Technology Innovation Management Review, 10*(7), 28–40.

Hoskisson, R. E., Eden, L., Lau, C. M., & Wright, M. (2000). Strategy in emerging economies. *Academy of Management Journal, 43*(3), 249–267.

Johanson, J., & Vahlne, J. (1977). The internationalization process of the firm. A model of knowledge development and increasing foreign market commitments. *Journal of International Business Studies, 8*, 23–32.

Luo, Y. (2021). New OLI advantages in digital globalization. *International Business Review, 30*, 1. https://doi.org/10.1016/j.ibusrev.2021.101797

Mathews, J. (2006). Dragon multinationals: New players in 21st century globalization. *Asia Pacific Journal of Management, 23*(1), 5–27.

Mathews, J. (2017). Dragon multinationals powered by linkage, leverage and learning: A review and development. *Asia Pacific Journal of Management, 34*, 769–777.

McDonald, F., & Burton, F. (2002). *International business.* Thomson.

Meyer, K., & Peng, M. (2016). Theoretical foundations of emerging economy business research. *Journal of International Business Studies, 47*, 3–22. https://doi.org/10.1057/jibs.2015.34

Ojala, A., Evers, N., & Sousa, C. (2022). Digitalisation, digital services and companies´ internationalisation. In *Sustainable international business models in a digitally transformed world.* Routledge.

Oliveira, R., Figueira, A., & Pinhanez, M. (2018). Uppsala model: A contingent theory to explain the rise of EMNEs. *Revista Eletrônica de Negócios Internacionais, 13*(2), 30–42.

Peng, M., Lebedev, S., Vlas, C., Wang, J., & Shay, J. (2018). The growth of the firm in (and out of) emerging economies. *Asia Pacific Journal of Management, 35*(4), 829–857.

Porter, M. (1998). Clusters and competition: New agendas for companies, governments, and institutions. In M. Porter (Ed.), *On competition.* Harvard Business School Press.

Ramamurti, R. (2012). What is really different about emerging market multinationals? *Global Strategy Journal, 2*(1), 41–47.

Rottig, D. (2016). Institutions and emerging markets: Effects and implications for multinational corporations. *International Journal of Emerging Markets, 11*(1), 2–17.

Schmidt, E. (2015). Speech at the World Economic Forum.

Strange, R., & Zucchella, A. (2017). Industry 4.0, global value chains and international business. *Multinational Business Review, 25*(4), 1. https://doi.org/10.1108/MBR-05-2017-0028

Teece, D., Pisano, G., & Shuen, A. (1997). Dynamic capabilities and strategic management. *Strategic Management Journal, 19*(7), 509–533.

Trust, G. (2022). Bizarrap & Quevedo's 'Bzrp Music Sessions, Vol. 52' Doubles Up Again Atop Billboard Global Charts. Retrieved from https://finance.yahoo.com/news/bizarrap-quevedo-bzrp-music-sessions-201451614.html?guccounter=1&guce_referrer=aHR0cHM6Ly93d3cuZ29vZ2xlLmNvbbS8&guce_referrer_sig=AQAAAF56_Trp7z0arRFR9jANiPPq6Rp7RsUWW0oKY_FLLkyC0yPqy3ScESa4Rb8XFKjfKFnea0Y4hW0eOrlxWDRlkp5XiUf3pX39NreTFtEPzg6snTIxMGtANU5G6Gqf2Hti6YjI1WTa5NbvDdlcwXE_dAcwHLbq4xWpYQs4lJChm59w

WTO. (2022). Statistics on trade in commercial services. Retrieved from https://www.wto.org/english/res_e/statis_e/tradeserv_stat_e.htm

4

Platforms and International Business

Abstract The chapter analyses the impact of digital platforms in the international expansion of businesses and discusses how they are shaping international business decisions, as well as the international strategy of companies. It also focuses on the key role they are having in the international expansion of small and medium enterprises. The discussion shows that platforms are having a positive impact on companies in the following areas: (i) they help companies to minimize the transaction costs of operating internationally; and not only that, they do this without the need for firms to internalize these transaction costs, (ii) they are changing consumption patterns and therefore opening new markets and demand both domestically and internationally, and (iii) they have been vital in reducing the liability of foreignness as they provide almost direct access to the final consumer regardless of where the producer is located. Challenges and future directions are also discussed, and examples are provided to illustrate the discussion.

Keywords Digital platforms • International expansion • International growth • SMEs

© The Author(s), under exclusive license to Springer Nature Switzerland AG 2023
G. Fornes, M. Altamira, *Digitalization, Technology and Global Business*,
https://doi.org/10.1007/978-3-031-33111-4_4

*"The advance of technology is based on making it fit in so that you don't
really even notice it, so it's part of everyday life"*
—*Bill Gates*, Co-founder of *Microsoft*

4.1 Introduction

Digital Platforms are "technology-based business models that connect
different users and interests while facilitating value-creating exchanges
that happen online" (Cennamo & Santalo, 2013: 1331). They enhance
the exchange of information, services, and goods, leveraging the participating community by providing added value to everyone participating in
the ecosystem. There are many different types of platforms, including
e-commerce, social media management, marketing automation, and
sales, among others; all meet different needs and target different contexts,
and all make products, services, and information widely available.
Benefits of platforms for companies include cost reductions through process automation, optimization of resources, and an increase of the visibility of the company and the brand with a positive impact on revenues.

The adoption of digital platforms, especially by non-digital firms, is a
recent phenomenon and, therefore, research and evidence about their
role and impact on international business is in its early stages. Most of the
studies developed in the area to date have analyzed digital platforms from
an information systems perspective and with a focus on their technical
side. From a business perspective the focus since the 2000s has been more
on the role of the Internet in the international performance of firms with
a focus on the development of the company's website and information
sharing (see for example (Barrutia & Echebarria, 2007; Costa et al., 2016;
Loane, 2005; Petersen et al., 2002; Rhee, 2005)).

In addition, most of the available knowledge in the field has been
developed in the context of the Asia Pacific Region (APAC), with a large
number of studies developed in China, the country being the largest
ecommerce market in the world (Luo et al., 2019). This is somewhat
expected as by 2023 retail ecommerce sales in Asia-Pacific are projected
to be greater than the rest of the world combined due to a rapid urbaniza-
tion and technological advancements in countries such as Vietnam,

Thailand, and Malaysia (Manisha, 2022). Most of the studies are developed in the context of small and medium-sized enterprises (Costa et al., 2019; Hervé et al., 2020; Huijun & Fiona, 2022; Jean & Kim, 2020) as these types of companies are anticipated to be the ones that will benefit the most from platforms to expand their activities.

The present chapter intends to analyze the impact of digital platforms in the international expansion of businesses. It reflects on how platforms are shaping international business decisions, as well as the international strategy of companies, with a special focus on their relevance for small and medium enterprises (SMEs). The chapter concludes with a discussion and application of the analysis, where case studies and examples are presented.

4.2   The Role of Digital Platforms in International Business

Digital platforms are playing a central role in today's digital, data-rich, and interconnected economy. Moreover, international trade of good and services has experienced major changes due to the impact of both digitalization (as analyzed in previous chapters) and the growth of digital platforms. This has become even more evident during the Covid-19 pandemic, when companies have seen their B2B and B2C relationships seriously damaged due to travel and personal movement restrictions. In this context, digitalization, the adoption of digital resources, and the development and participation in digital platforms have become an imperative for all types of companies from different industries and sectors to successfully navigate through the increasingly interconnected, digitalized, and challenging global markets.

The Internet and advances in information technology (IT) have transformed international business operations enhancing cross border coordination among firms through platforms (Jean et al., 2020). Digital technologies such as smartphones or the Internet of Things (IoT) have allowed an increasing number of industries (beyond digitally mature industries) to embrace digitalization and adopt digital platforms, making it easier to connect different actors in real time in different locations (Evans & Schmalensee, 2016). In addition, platforms are based on and offer companies lower transaction costs and fewer capacity constraints. Therefore, they can be expanded and scaled up rapidly, often with low required investments (Autio & Zander, 2016; Van Alstyne et al., 2016). Furthermore, digital platforms support information sharing, collaboration and collective action among actors involved in international transactions (Spagnoletti et al., 2015). In this sense, a key characteristic of platforms is their flexibility and efficiency to connect with consumers or other businesses allowing a more rapid development of B2B and C2C relations than with traditional channels and tools. Consequently, they help firms to expand their national and international operations while interacting and keeping up with the changing preferences, thoughts, and perceptions of their consumers, partners, and stakeholder all around the globe.

Indeed, in recent years, digital platforms have been playing an increasingly important role in the international expansion of companies, beyond digital native global firms. Platforms have demonstrated to help to coordinate transactions among users all around the globe, reducing distance-related costs and risks, helping companies to expand their business internationally, and speeding up their internationalization process while at the same time creating new opportunities (Stallkamp & Schotter, 2021). Bughin et al. (2019) showed that more than half of incumbent firms operating in sectors going digital have adopted third-party platforms and that a large number of MNEs from almost every sector or industry are developing their own ones. Despite the different adoption rate in different sectors (55% of pharmaceutical companies use platforms versus 95% of retail banks, and 65% of B2B companies versus 85% B2C companies) this confirms that the use of platforms has also become an imperative for incumbent firms in order to increase international presence and global reach, platforms allowing companies to merge and combine individual services to a full-service offering. As a consequence, the major benefit for MNEs is the speed of accessing new markets and the capacity to reach exponential growth, becoming a competitive necessity to operate in the international scene and become global players.

Platforms can take several forms, from innovation platforms of knowledge sharing to cloud storage. However transaction platforms are the ones considered the most relevant and also the ones with the strongest impact on international business and trade (Li et al., 2022). This type of platform, that can be two-sided or multi-sided, refers to platforms such as e-commerce platforms, searchers, e-payment platforms, or social media platforms. Their primary goal is to facilitate commercial transactions, marketing, and sales of products to the global market; they also capture, transmit, and monetize data on their behavior (Yablonsky, 2018).

For example, digital e-commerce platforms such as eBay, Amazon, Alibaba, or Etsy connect buyers and sellers, including B2B, B2C and C2C, for a wide range of products and services. They allow companies to sell their products and services to a large number of customers at a lower cost than conventional retail selling channels, offering companies a uniform platform with automatic process of transactions, 24/7 end-to-end available service. Moreover, the emergence of cross-border e-commerce platforms has allowed instant global reach, faster positioning, efficient international brand and presence, and lower barrier entries, enabling firms to achieve a faster international expansion (Jin & Hurd, 2018). Social media networks such as Facebook and LinkedIn have also proven to offer low cost/efficient means to expand international companies that connect producers with international consumers; they have also replaced functions of export intermediaries. This is particularly relevant in the context of small and medium enterprises (SMEs) as they usually face more challenges, barriers, and cost restrictions than MNEs in international contexts (Fornes & Cardoza, 2019; Jean & Kim, 2020).

For a successful impact on the company and an efficient development of platforms in the medium and long term, firms should go beyond the decision of adoption and also carefully analyze and define the time and efforts required in the development and the management of platforms in international markets. At the end of the day, platforms are major sales channels and as such they impact the positioning, image, and resources of firms.

Furthermore, it seems imperative for managers to study the intensity, persistence, and scope of the attention needed towards digital platforms in their international operations. Li et al. (2022) have analyzed the impact of digital platforms on the international strategy of MNEs with regards to these three variables. They showed that companies with intense and persistent attention towards digital platforms are more likely to sell more internationally compared to those with a more diversified scope. Also, the geographic, psychic, and cultural distance between headquarters and international subsidiaries affect the impact of platforms on international sales. Indeed, the intensity of use of platforms is diminished the further the subsidiaries are located and the more culturally different the market is. In sum, international managers should pay intense and persistence attention to platforms but should also recognize that subsidiaries in remote locations might pose challenges that "distract and dilute the attention of managers at the company's headquarters, which in turn may diminish the focus on the MNE's digital platforms" (Li et al., 2022).

In fact, despite the multiple benefits of platforms for MNEs, several difficulties and challenges still arise in host markets. Managers must pay relevant and sustained attention to their digital platforms so that they can analyze, define, and implement digital platform strategies suitable to their international scope and goals, while generating benefits and reducing costs (Bughin et al., 2019). The most common risks faced by MNEs are usually issues related to data security and privacy, technological complexity, or copyright risks (Li et al., 2022; 簡睿哲, Jean, Kim, Zhou ,, & Cavusgil, 2021). These risks are more evident in the case of Western MNEs expanding to emerging markets (China for example) where the institutional environment is relatively weak and more informal than the one found at home, with several information systems problems (for example, comprehensive, objective and reliable data not widely available) and misguided regulations (Cardoza et al., 2015; Rottig, 2016).

In this sense, failure to deal with these issues can lead to a loss in digital platform engagement, wasted time and resources, and loss of brand reputation. Risks related to the complexity of the product specificity can lead to a more difficult and costly adoption by consumers. The high competition and uncertainty linked to institutional voids in EMs might have also negative impact on the expected performance from the use of digital platforms, mainly on sales performance and market penetration in the host market, and therefore on the international strategy and international scope of the firm (Jean et al., 2020). It is in this context that managers should therefore carefully assess whether the use of the digital platform would be worth it, the type of platform to be used abroad, along with a specific suitable strategy for the host market.

All in all, it can be concluded that digital platforms, especially transaction platforms, have become a must-have tool for businesses, incumbent and born-digital, operating in both digitalized and less digitalized sectors and industries. Despite the risks that MNEs can face in international business contexts, platforms have been demonstrated to enhance the digitalization strategy of firms, support their internationalization strategy, speed up their internationalization process, enhance market penetration, and boost sales in host markets.

4.3   The Role of Digital Platforms in the International Expansion of SMEs

Similar to what happens with multinationals, as previously analyzed in this chapter, SMEs are also increasingly engaging with digitalization. Innovation, which is at the core of SMEs and entrepreneurship, supports a better and more efficient adaptation to the digital environment (Hervé et al., 2020). In this sense, the use of digital platforms has been demonstrated to enhance innovation opportunities and access to innovation assets to SMEs while increasing their productivity. Indeed, the use of digital platforms is playing a fundamental role in SMEs' domestic and international growth; some of the activities developed through the use of digital platforms include marketing operations, e-commerce, service delivery, financing and payment, and research and development operations (OECD XE "OECD", 2022a).

International expansion requires an effort in resources and the ability to process large amounts of data, information, and knowledge. Given the limited initial resources of SMEs and the resulting challenges to target new international markets, these firms usually rely on external networks to develop their international operations (Costa et al., 2019; Huijun & Fiona, 2022). Consequently, the rise of digital platforms plays a relevant role in supporting the internationalization process of SMEs and offers significant benefits for their international operations and sales.

Costa et al. (2019) analyzed the extent to which digital platforms, developed by business associations dedicated to support SMEs, promote the international expansion of these firms. Based on the outcomes of this anaylisis, digital platforms (i) promote capacity building for international expansion in the specific sector, (ii) support companies in getting relevant information about international markets (including business information to define the strategy), (iii) help companies to identify business opportunities and increase their visibility abroad, (iv) facilitate collaborative networks, and (v) offer a single point of contact for the different actors. As a consequence, digital platforms play a key role in helping SMEs increase their customer base, enhancing their regional and global reach. They provide the necessary infrastructure to connect buyers and sellers while delivering the offer around the globe; they also manage B2B and B2C relationships in an efficient manner.

Digital platforms have also been demonstrated to facilitate SMEs' exports. The Internet has been used by many SMEs as a low cost means to enter international markets as it facilitates the development of B2B and B2C contacts in host markets and allows international consumers to become aware more rapidly of the brand. Platforms also replace some of the activities performed by export intermediaries and representatives of the firm (Costa et al., 2016). This clearly represents an efficient export channel option for SMEs, usually dealing with limited resources (Cho & Tansuhaj, 2013).

Social network platforms, for example, offer a low-cost alternative to contact new foreign partners or consumers. In this context, Jean and Kim (2020) have analyzed the impact of platform capabilities (defined as the ability of SMEs to use platforms for exporting purposes) in export performance. They analyzed the mediation role of export marketing capabilities and demonstrated the positive effect of platform use on export performance. They found that platforms become more relevant the higher the product complexity is; this is because platforms facilitate the exports of these products by improving communication and targeting the relevant consumers in host markets. However, in environments with strong and intense competition, results suggest that platforms can be less effective as they are vulnerable to competitive forces such as price war or product imitation, the company's website being the most efficient tool for information, therefore reducing uncertainty and creating trust.

Furthermore, digital platforms support market entry of SMEs in host markets. As previously mentioned, most SMEs find resource constraints when entering new markets. Firms need to make financial investments in marketing and brand awareness and usually need a local team to develop market knowledge and to target the products locally. These activities represent a huge effort for SMEs in terms of investments. In addition, they are also affected by the liability of foreignness, making the international expansion even more costly. In this context, the use of digital platforms helps to reduce entry barriers (Huijun & Fiona, 2022), especially when these firms enter markets characterized by less mature business and institutional environments (Child & Marinova, 2014; Child & Rodrigues, 2005; Fornes et al., 2021).

In a context of international expansion of SMEs to China, Huijun and Fiona (2022) showed that the use of local platforms helped to reduce the stages that companies usually need along with the related efforts and costs to establish a subsidiary; for example, the administrative work involved in the registration process of a firm in the country. In addition, digital platforms also helped to reduce marketing and branding investments, minimizing the psychological distance and consumers' lack of knowledge, familiarity, and trust on the foreign company; although they also found that the support of locally-based human resources is still key. In any case, the use of local digital platforms is a positive endorsement for the foreign company in the local market. Finally, through digital platforms SMEs have a quicker and more efficient access to a large consumer segment, speeding up the penetration in the market.

However, digital platforms pose several challenges to SMEs. Jean and Kim (2020) conceptualized platform risks as the opportunistic behaviors, threats, and uncertainty when using platforms in the exchange process with foreign customers. Example of risks are price information misuse by competitors, which can translate into negative relations with consumers and distributors due to pricing complexities, foreign market competition and regulations, domestic institution voids, and market uncertainty. Another known issue for SMEs is the limited resources, in this case the required financial and human resources for a successful use of a digital platform in the international context. The initial costs and the resources needed to maintain the platform with updated information, constantly managing information communication and attracting new customers, may be a high barrier for digital platform adoption (Costa et al., 2019). This becomes even more challenging in the case of SMEs setting up their own platforms, which usually involves higher complexities and costs, and lower margins in the short term. At first sight MNEs have an advantage in this sense, although SMEs should be able to leverage on their flexibility, adaptability and focus on the activities that interact with customers and business partners.

Another major difficulty (which also affects MNEs (Li et al., 2022)) relates to data protection risk and digital security. While using digital platforms, firms are sharing relevant and sensitive data including clients and consumers´ statistics, data and information, or relevant information about the business. In this context, cybersecurity may become a major weakness in the business model of SMEs as they need high investments and attract people with very specific skills; the challenge is that SMEs usually have difficulties in accessing this type of resource (OECD XE "OECD", 2022a).

Similarly, SMEs also face risks related to the protection of business ideas and/or business models and the potential misleading/unfair competition. While digital platforms facilitate the development of an international network, SMEs face the risk of not only other SMEs using their business ideas, but what would be even worse, of bigger and more powerful companies with more financial and human resources using this information to strengthen their offer and therefore outcompete the SME.

In order to address the potential challenges and risks, and to provide with recommendations, Costa et al. (2019) have analyzed the requirements and features that digital platforms or designers of digital platforms need to consider. These recommendations are aimed at supporting the international expansion of SMEs which are grouped into four categories: (i) Information; digital platforms should allow SMEs to securely share information while having access to relevant information about the market (including legal and market conditions) as well as about possible collaborators; (ii): Collaboration; SMEs should be able to benefit from access to joint international business opportunities including logistics sharing through digital platforms, (iii) Communication; social networks are key tools for SMEs in the international context as well as platforms for marketing and media communication, so their access to these platforms should be widely available, and finally (iv) other requirements such as platforms being user-friendly, cost efficient, flexible and easily to adapt to the specific needs of the company in the international context.

In conclusion, in our digital era, most SMEs face the challenge of embracing digital platforms. They promote innovation rapidly due to the flexibility of these firms and to their agility in their decision-making processes (Xuemei et al., 2022). In international markets, platforms provide an efficient means to access new markets, helping SMEs to overcome barriers such as limited information access, difficulties in finding international opportunities or international business partners, lack of financial resources, inefficiencies of human resources management, the liability of foreignness, among others (OECD XE "OECD" , 2022b). They have therefore become, despite the challenges and risks (especially in the context of data security), a key element for SMEs competing beyond their domestic market.

4.4   Application and Discussion

The full impact and implications of platforms are still to be seen. For example, the eWTP (World Trade Platform), hatched by Jack Ma (Alibaba founder) (WTO, 2017) and included in the communiqué of the Group of 20 (G20) in Hangzhou (G20 2016, 2016), has 500 million users and expects to reach 2 billion by the end of the decade. The eWTP is a "private sector-led, multi-stakeholder initiative to promote public-private collaboration and dialogue in support of inclusive global trade" (eWTP, 2022) and intends to create a set of international rules to reduce traditional barriers for commerce and as a consequence improve SMEs' opportunities to carry out business overseas. To achieve this, it works with governments in the creation of a stable, reliable, and efficient trade system. This private-led platform is in the driving seat while governments play a supporting role (Lucas, 2017); this in itself is unique.

eWTP has already developed agreements in Belgium, China, Ethiopia, Malaysia, Rwanda, Mexico, and Thailand. In these countries it cooperates with local authorities and invests in establishing services and logistic facilities to provide firms with one-stop digital solutions for customs clearance and logistics. eWTP also offers information and insights on trade policies of different target markets along with support for its members to carry out international trade in an efficient way; this leads to companies dealing in a smooth way with the traditional customs, tariffs, and non-tariffs barriers.

"Thanks to the eWTP initiative—which Rwanda joined in 2018—Rwandan businesses can sell directly to Chinese consumers via Tmall Global, one of Alibaba Group's cross-border online shopping platforms. Being able to sell directly to shoppers online without the need to set up physical shops, create a local website, or invest in marketing, has been transformative for businesses and farmers alike. For every kilo of coffee sold through Tmall Global under the eWTP initiative, farmers in Rwanda can earn US$4 more than what they normally earn through the traditional model of farmer to middleman to foreign brand distributor and finally retail" (Fortune, 2022).

The example above shows how platforms amplify the reach of companies and therefore how they can help firms to grow by accessing new and diverse international markets. The main help is in the reduction of the transaction costs, which in itself challenges the premise that international companies need to internalize them (rather than relying on a third-party to achieve the same). They do this by providing almost all (if not all) the necessary infrastructure (physical and digital) for warehousing and distribution, payment methods, transportation, customs clearance, etc. They also support with lowering the liability of foreignness, as they provide an umbrella brand where products and services are sold (along with the associated trust from consumers, legal protection, and efficient customer service), access to consumption trends, and information to identify new markets (Fornes & Cardoza, 2019). As a US-based consumer put it, "I don't mind if it is made in China or somewhere else, I buy from Amazon and I trust them, their service, and their accountability".

Another impact of platforms is that they are transforming consumers from owners to licensees. In most major cities it is now possible to enjoy a bicycle, an e-scooter, an apartment, and even a car for only a low percentage of the cost of owning the asset. The same for services, movies, music, or audiobooks/ebooks, they can be accessed almost everywhere for a relatively small fee (lower than the acquisition cost of the hardware that contain them) (Thornhill, 2021). This has been possible because platforms have tapped into a new demand, multiplying the number of consumers, which at the same time provides more opportunities for member companies to access these markets.

An example of how platforms tap into new demand is Money Heist [1]. This Spanish heist crime drama television series was first aired on traditional TV in 2017 with a strong debut but with declining numbers after a few weeks, in fact it was cancelled and considered a failure by the broadcaster (Díaz-Guerra, 2019). It was then sold as part of a package to Netflix, and by 2018 the series was the most-watched non-English-language series and one of the most-watched series overall on the platform. The main reasons explaining this success are that Netflix changed consumption habits of series viewers by offering the possibility of binge-watching rather than the traditional weekly episodes (Sola Gimferrer, 2019) and also that thanks to the possibilities offered by the platform it is accessible to many different profile groups, beyond those on prime-time traditional TV (Avendaño, 2019).

Finally, an unforeseen consequence of platforms has been the access to funding. The great majority of sales on Amazon's marketplace (US$300 billion in 2020) come from independent firms; this means that companies/products that are in the top listings of Amazon can get millions in sales. Investors are seeking this type of seller to strengthen their supply chains, sharpen marketing activities, launch new products, increase margins, and tap into new markets. In fact, during 2020 and the first half of 2021, an estimate of US$7 billion has been invested in successful Amazon sellers (Lee, 2021). As a consequence of this, companies and in particular SMEs overcome finding sources of funding for expansion, one of the major barriers for international growth (Cardoza & Fornes, 2011; Leonidou, 2004).

---

[1] https://www.netflix.com/es-en/title/80192098

4.5   Concluding Remarks

Previous chapters have shown how digitalization and technology have impacted the operation of companies and in particular their international expansion. This chapter has focused on one of the key pivots of this impact, platforms. As seen throughout the chapter, platforms are the main element supporting companies, especially SMEs, to overcome most of the barriers usually associated with internationalization.

Platforms helped companies to minimize the transaction costs of operating internationally; and not only that, they do this without the need for firms to internalize these transaction costs. This is because they provide most of the resources needed to serve diverse markets in an efficient way; this at the same time allows enterprises to focus on their competitive advantages rather than on also developing new capabilities to operate internationally.

Platforms are also changing consumption patterns and as a consequence opening new markets and demand both domestically and internationally. E-commerce sales as a percentage of total retail sales worldwide have grown from 7% in 2015 to 20% in 2020 and they are expected to reach 24% in 2026 (Statista, 2022); this change in patterns was accelerated by the Covid 19-related restrictions. The interesting thing to observe is that this growth has not all/always been to the detriment of traditional retail (although there are some industries that have suffered major changes in consumption patterns, like banking or tourism); platforms have found new sources of demand for member companies through the use of technology to provide new products services. They have achieved this by offering more personalized products/services, sharing assets, pricing based on usage, and creating more collaborative ecosystems (Kavadias et al., 2016).

Platforms have also been vital in reducing the barriers, timeframes, and investments to operate overseas. This reduction in the liability of foreignness has been possible as they provide almost direct access to the final consumer regardless of where the producer is located. They also provide a trusted umbrella brand, legal protection, and infrastructure to provide local customer service. And as a consequence of this possibility for exponential growth, platforms have put thousands of companies in the spotlight, most previously unknown to consumers and investors, to receive funding to improve their operations and therefore further reduce the barriers to growth. In short, platforms are one of the most important levers for companies to expand their business in an increasingly digitalized market.

References

Avendaño, T. (2019, 2 August 2019). 'La casa de papel' logra más de 34 millones de espectadores y refuerza la estrategia internacional de Netflix. *El Pais*. Retrieved from https://elpais.com/cultura/2019/08/01/television/1564671328_371797.html

Barrutia, J. M., & Echebarria, C. (2007). A new internet driven internationalisation framework. *The Service Industries Journal, 27*(7), 923–946.

Bughin, J., Catlin, T., & Dietz, M. (2019). The right digital-platform strategy. *McKinsey Quarterly, 2*, 1–4.

Cardoza, G., & Fornes, G. (2011). The internationalisation of SMEs from China: The case of Ningxia Hui autonomous region. *Asia Pacific Journal of Management, 28*(4), 737–759.

Cardoza, G., Fornes, G., Li, P., Xu, N., & Xu, S. (2015). China goes global: Public policies' influence on small- and medium-sized enterprises' international expansion. *Asia Pacific Business Review, 21*(2), 188–210.

Child, J., & Marinova, S. (2014). The role of contextual combinations in the globalization of Chinese firms. *Management and Organization Review, 10*(3), 347–371.

Child, J., & Rodrigues, S. (2005). The internationalization of Chinese firms: A case for theoretical extension? *Management and Organization Review, 1*(3), 381–410.

Costa, E., Soares, A. L., & De Sousa, J. P. (2016). Information, knowledge and collaboration management in the internationalisation of SMEs: A systematic literature review. *International Journal of Information Management, 36*(4), 557–569.

Costa, E., Soares, A., & Pinho de Sousa, J. (2019). On the use of digital platforms to support SME internationalization in the context of industrial business associations. doi: https://doi.org/10.4018/978-1-5225-6225-2.ch004.

Díaz-Guerra, I. (2019, 12 September 2019). Javier Gómez Santander: "Los españoles no somos un buen ejército, pero como guerrilla somos la hostia". *El Mundo*. Retrieved from https://www.elmundo.es/papel/cultura/2019/09/12/ 5d791951fc6c8337538b45fe.html

eWTP. (2022). Who we are. Retrieved from https://www.ewtp.org/

Fornes, G., & Cardoza, G. (2019). Internationalization of Chinese SMEs: The perception of disadvantages of foreignness. *Emerging Markets Finance and Trade, 55*(9), 2086–2105.

Fornes, G., Cardoza, G., & Altamira, M. (2021). Do political and business relations help emerging markets' SMEs in their national and international expansion? Evidence from Brazil and China. *International Journal of Emerging Markets*. doi: https://doi.org/10.1108/IJOEM-01-2020-0058

Fortune. (2022). The electronic World Trade Platform: making global trade more inclusive. *Fortune*. Retrieved from https://brand-studio.fortune.com/ alibaba-group/making-global-trade-more-inclusive/?prx_t=dT8HAzi5SAoP EQA&spm=a2o7pe.23809426

G20 2016. (2016). G20 Leaders' Communique Hangzhou Summit. Retrieved from http://www.g20chn.org/English/Dynamic/201609/t20160906_3396. html

Hervé, A., Schmitt, C., & Baldegger, R. (2020). Internationalization and digitalization: Applying digital technologies to the internationalization process of small and medium-sized enterprises. *Technology Innovation Management Review, 10*(7), 28–40.

Huijun, J., & Fiona, H. (2022). Exploring the impact of digital platforms on SME internationalization: New Zealand SMEs use of the Alibaba platform for Chinese market entry. *Journal of Asia-Pacific Business, 19*(2), 72–95. https://doi.org/10.1080/10599231.2018.1453743

Jean, R.-J. B., & Kim, D. (2020). Internet and SMEs' internationalization: The role of platform and website. *Journal of International Management, 26*(1), 100690. https://doi.org/10.1016/j.intman.2019.100690

Jean, R.-J. B., Kim, D., & Cavusgil, E. (2020). Antecedents and outcomes of digital platform risk for international new ventures' internationalization. *Journal of World Business, 55*(1), 101021. https://doi.org/10.1016/j. jwb.2019.101021

Jin, H., & Hurd, F. (2018). Exploring the impact of digital platforms on SME internationalization: New Zealand SMEs use of the Alibaba platform for Chinese market entry. *Journal of Asia-Pacific Business, 19*(2), 72–95. https:// doi.org/10.1080/10599231.2018.1453743

Kavadias, S., Ladas, K., & Loch, C. (2016). The transformative business model. How to tell if you have one. *Harvard Business Review, October.*

Lee, D. (2021, 29 July 2021). A Tesla for every referral' as start-ups buy Amazon's top sellers. *Financial Times.*

Leonidou, L. (2004). An analysis of the barriers hindering small business export development. *Journal of Small Business Management, 42*(3), 279–302.

Li, J., Pan, Y., Yang, Y., & Tse, C. H. (2022). Digital platform attention and international sales: An attention-based view. *Journal of International Business Studies.* https://doi.org/10.1057/s41267-022-00528-4

Loane, S. (2005). The role of the internet in the internationalisation of small and medium sized companies. *Journal of International Entrepreneurship, 3*(4), 263–277.

Lucas, L. (2017, 22 March 2017). Alibaba kicks off ambitious plan for frontier-free global trade. *Financial Times.*

Luo, X., Wang, Y., & Zhang, X. (2019). E-Commerce development and household consumption growth in China. *World Bank Policy Research Working Paper*(8810).

Manisha, N. (2022). Asian Development Bank, Asian economic integration report 2022: Advancing digital services trade in Asia and the Pacific, Asian Development Bank, 2022, 300 pp., \$51 (paperback). ISBN: 978-92-9269-361-9 (print), ISBN: 978-92-9269-362-6 (electronic), 978-92-9269-363-3 (eBook). *Journal of Asian Economic Integration, 4*(2), 211–213. https://doi.org/10.1177/26316846221107416

OECD. (2022a). *OECD studies on SMEs and entrepreneurship.* OECDilibrary.

OECD. (2022b). SMEs and enterpreneurship. Retrieved from https://www.oecd.org/cfe/smes/

Petersen, B., Welch, L. S., & Liesch, P. W. (2002). *The internet and foreign market expansion by firms* (pp. 207–221). MIR: Management International Review.

Rhee, J. H. (2005). The internet era and the international expansion process: The moderating role of absorptive capacity. *MIR: Management International Review, 1,* 277–306.

Rottig, D. (2016). Institutions and emerging markets: Effects and implications for multinational corporations. *International Journal of Emerging Markets, 11*(1), 2–17.

Sola Gimferrer, P. (2019, 19/7/2019). Las claves del éxito de La casa de papel. *La Vanguardia.* Retrieved from https://www.lavanguardia.com/series/netflix/20190719/463580297705/la-casa-de-papel-claves-exito-serie-netflix.html

Spagnoletti, P., Resca, A., & Lee, G. (2015). A design theory for digital platforms supporting online communities: A multiple case study. *Journal of Information Technology, 30*, 1. https://doi.org/10.1057/jit.2014.37

Stallkamp, M., & Schotter, A. P. (2021). Platforms without borders? The international strategies of digital platform firms. *Global Strategy Journal, 11*(1), 58–80. https://doi.org/10.1002/gsj.1336

Statista. (2022). E-commerce as percentage of total retail sales worldwide from 2015 to 2021, with forecasts from 2022 to 2026. Retrieved from https://www.statista.com/statistics/534123/e-commerce-share-of-retail-sales-worldwide/

Xuemei, X., Yuhang, H., Alistair, A., & Samuel, R.-N. (2022). Digital platforms and SMEs' business model innovation: Exploring the mediating mechanisms of capability reconfiguration. *International Journal of Information Management, 65*, 102513. https://doi.org/10.1016/j.ijinfomgt.2022.102513

Yablonsky, S. (2018). Transaction platforms: Fintech platforms. In *Multi-sided platforms (MSPs) and sharing strategies in the digital economy: Emerging research and opportunities* (pp. 113–133). Hershey, PA, USA.

簡睿哲, Jean, B. R.-J., Kim, D., Zhou, K. Z., & Cavusgil, S. T. (2021). E-Platform use and exporting in the context of Alibaba: A signaling theory perspective. *Journal of International Business Studies*. Retrieved from http://nccur.lib.nccu.edu.tw/handle/140.119/135880.

5

Artificial Intelligence and International Business

Abstract Artificial Intelligence (AI) has been increasingly adopted in the business operations of companies over the last 15+ and has shown a positive contribution to business performance while supporting international expansion of firms. In this sense, the chapter critically analyzes the impact of AI on the current international business scenario, discusses the challenges presented for companies and society and presents the future trends and expected impacts of this technology. The discussion shows that while AI increases productivity, facilitates cross-cultural communication (and as a consequence, international negotiations), and enables knowledge management exchange, among other benefits for the international expansion of firms, AI's real impact in international business is developing gradually and will only be evident in the medium term. The chapter also analyzes today's major challenges: (i) widening the gap in the adoption and implementation of AI among countries, companies, and workers, and (ii) adapting trade rules and regulations to a context increasingly influenced by new technologies.

Keywords Artificial intelligence • International expansion • Privacy • Technology gap

G. Fornes, M. Altamira, *Digitalization, Technology and Global Business*,
https://doi.org/10.1007/978-3-031-33111-4_5

"Technology is best when it brings people together"
—Matt Mullenweg developer of WordPress and founder of Automattic

5.1 Introduction

Artificial intelligence (AI) is a major contributor to today's accelerated sixth wave of innovation and technology, creating an increasing impact on businesses from a variety of industries. AI is not a new technology, indeed, it has existed as a concept since the 60s, but its impact has become tangible in the last five years as a source and driver for innovation through automation of systems and data processing (Neufeld, 2021). The main characteristic of this technology is that it reproduces and responds to some aspects of human intelligence (Andrea & Andrea De, 2021), usually underlying other technologies such as deep learning, natural language processing, computer vision, or supervised and unsupervised machine learning, among others. AI systems are designed to operate with a certain degree of autonomy, and are able to make predictions, recommendations and decisions for a set of humanly defined objectives in a given environment or scenario (Ferencz et al., 2022). They are able (i) to process natural language, (ii) to represent knowledge (iii) to develop automated reasoning and (iv) to demonstrate machine learning capabilities (Loureiro et al., 2021).

AI functions with data and algorithms that can be usually found in software used by hardware such as robots, applications with Internet of Things (IoT), cars, or medical devices. Some examples of AI application include autonomous cars, medical diagnosis, smart manufacturing, and robotics and is used across a variety of industries and sectors from agriculture to education, to provide descriptive, predictive, prescriptive and prognostics analytics targeted solutions (Chappell, 2020). In this context, it is evident that AI is having a great impact on business, trade, economics and society, reshaping interactions, transactions, and relationships among different stakeholders, not only in the local, but in the international context as well.

In recent years, AI has experienced an impressive evolution, contributing to innovative solutions to complex issues in the international business context (Loureiro et al., 2021; Ruiz-Real et al., 2021). The growing interest in business comes from the ability of this technology to manage large amounts of data in a short period of time and in any form, allowing to systematize and classify widely available but disaggregated data for rapid and efficient decision-making processes in the entire global value chain. Despite the adoption rate differing among industries, sectors and markets (Bughin et al., 2018), the use and implementation of AI in business will continue to increase at the time the contribution of this new disruptive technology to the economic activities and competitive advantage of international firms is realized (Ruiz-Real et al., 2021; Yogesh et al., 2021).

In this context, the present chapter intends to critically analyze the impact AI is having on the current business environment, on society, as well as on the international scene, contributing to enhance international companies' competitive positioning. The application and discussion section presents examples on how AI is improving business performance and also supporting the international expansion. The chapter also identifies challenges and discuss the future of this technology.

5.2 The Impact of Artificial Intelligence in the Business Environment and in Society

Artificial intelligence (AI) has been widely considered to be a general-purpose technology with a strong potential to foster innovation while helping companies to create value from data and to optimize costs (Ferencz et al., 2022). Today, AI can be categorized into two subfields: (i) Narrow AI and (ii) General AI. Narrow AI is designed to focus on and solve one unique given problem, and refers to the main current capabilities of AI and the technology commercially viable. Examples of Narrow AI include face and speech recognition, natural language procession, and self-driven cars. General AI, on the other hand, represents the future capabilities of AI, systems that would be able to develop a wide range of cognitive tasks like a human, including reasoning, developing creativity, and even expressing emotions (Ferencz et al., 2022; Melzer, 2018).

Data shows that AI application and implementation in the business environment is increasing. Today, 75% of organizations have adopted AI in at least one of their functions and are willing to increase its use in response to the Covid-19 environment. However, as stated above, the adoption rate differs among industries: high-tech and telecom companies are the leading adopters of AI with the automotive and assembly sector falling just behind; financial services and healthcare companies are still the laggards, mainly due to more complex legal and regulatory requirements (Balakrishnan et al., 2020). AI is a disruptive technological development that is making businesses adapt their operations models, as it has the power to create impact on the most basic functions of the firm. This is due mainly to the speed of data processing accelerating decision making processes that allow operational costs to be reduced (Ruiz-Real et al., 2021).

Nevertheless, it seems that companies are becoming familiar with the benefits of this technology, more specifically with its potential to improve productivity and efficiency while boosting competitive advantages. Indeed, AI systems are already offering real benefits and opportunities across a wide range of business contexts. Examples include, among others (Ferencz et al., 2022):

- Logistics: optimizing and predicting demand for a better warehouse management and organization of inventories.
- Transport: contributing to the development of safe autonomous cars and to the optimization of transportation routes and operations.
- Financial services: improving efficiency and personalization of financial products and operations, while detecting fraud.
- Professional services: increasing efficiency in daily tasks of professionals such as lawyers, engineers, and architects.
- Virtual assistants: empowering software that relies on natural language processing and able to respond to written or oral commands.

- Marketing and advertising: improving consumer experience and personalizing content, while making better predictions for tailored marketing actions.
- Agriculture: analyzing farm data and predicting the consequences of weather conditions, water usage or soil health.
- Health care: enhancing medical diagnostics, surgery procedures while preventing disease outbreaks.
- Language learning and automated translation: improving automated language learning, translation processes, and facilitating the automation of simple communications.

Loureiro et al. (2021) recently carried out a literature review of the state of the art of AI and analyzed the real impact the technology is having in organizations. According to their research, the impact can be framed within five main areas:

(i) work and labor relations: AI systems are transforming the nature of jobs and the relationships among workers. Despite some jobs being replaced by innovative AI systems (i.e., robots, platforms, among others), the adoption of AI, on the other hand, also represents new job opportunities for newly developed job positions related to AI. AI is also contributing to developing entrepreneurial capabilities in employees, improving persuading communication, formulating questions to promote problem solving, and fostering creativity,

(ii) manufacturing: AI is increasing the efficiency of the entire value chain, with a special impact on optimizing product definition tailored to the demand and on the quality of the outputs. A better warehouse management and efficiency in resources and operations is also being experienced in manufacturing companies,

(iii) knowledge management: AI is creating value through processes and strategies that enhance and facilitate the storing, sharing and creation of in-house knowledge. This has an impact on the innovation capabilities of companies, with a positive effect on the competitive advantage of the firm (Tidd & Bessant, 2020)

(iv) decision support: integrating human, technical and organizational systems, AI highly contributes to more efficient decision-making processes and therefore promotes a more efficient virtuous cycle of continuous improvement thanks to the inputs derived from AI systems, and finally

(v) fuzzy logic approach and risk management: an approach based on degrees of truth (as opposed to the usual true or false) that contributes to the overall process of quality improvement through risk management.

Moreover, the impact of AI systems and their applications are also becoming increasingly relevant at society and at individual level. Work displacements due to automation are expected to represent a third of the current job positions by 2030, but will also create new job opportunities, especially skilled technological profiles with more creative and cognitive orientated roles in support of AI technologies (Yogesh et al., 2021). On the other hand, it is also expected that in the near future and especially with the development of general AI, robots would be able to perform tasks with creativity and with the same level of intelligence as humans, being able to deliver greater value than persons through the delivery, for example, of highly personalized and customized services, although research shows that this event can be dysfunctional and that can create mental disorder and psychological issues in the population (Loureiro et al., 2021; Scoglio et al., 2019).

Also, the relationship between consumers and companies is changing along with consumers' behavior and consumption patterns. AI systems have demonstrated to be good at analyzing and predicting individual consumption and expenditure patterns. Consumers are therefore exposed to tailor-made recommendations and offers, with companies anticipating consumers' choices and developing the ability of influencing consumption patterns; social media is playing a relevant role in this. Finally, although in its early stages, AI is improving the efficiency of healthcare operations with better diagnosis and prevention capabilities. AI systems are expected to create a significant impact on patient care and wellbeing while saving operating costs and money (Marr, 2022). It seems therefore evident that life is and will continue to be influenced by AI, with major benefits for society.

With the increasing presence of AI systems, laws and regulations are to be adapted to the new reality; the challenge is how to ensure that new technologies are at the service of people, and not the opposite. Indeed, although AI offers many opportunities across a range of different applications and industries as mentioned above, it also raises a number of questions, especially with regards to governance structures, ethics, and regulations. Many companies have already adopted AI systems in some of their processes or activities, but most of them are not yet fully prepared for the various challenges presented by the technology (Accenture Research, 2021).

5.3 The Impact of AI in the International Business Environment

A new phase of globalization driven by AI is shaping today's international business context. Estimations show that AI will contribute with up to 16% ($13 trillion) to the global economy and up to 26% to global GDP by 2030 (Bughin et al., 2018). Digital technologies and AI in particular are accelerating the transition to service economies, increasing even more the international exchanges between markets and geographies. There is no doubt therefore that AI is affecting the type and quality of economic growth, transforming the international expansion of firms while creating vast implications for international trade.

In this context, AI is already contributing to companies' international expansion in several ways. First, it increases the productivity of companies adopting AI systems, which is associated with greater benefits from trade through exports (Ferencz et al., 2022), especially in data intensive sectors such as finance, insurance, or online platforms. Actually, in the case of online platforms, thanks to AI-developed translation services, digital platforms are key in the international growth and expansion of companies adopting them. For example, (Brynjolfsson et al., 2019) explained how a Chinese-based online platform helped to increase companies' sales in Latin America by 17.5% as a result of the implementation of a machine translation service.

Second, AI facilitates cross-cultural communication and improves international negotiations. AI systems promote and facilitate the access to valuable information, support a better analysis of economic trajectories under different assumptions and scenarios, and therefore ease the process of achieving a suitable outcome for both parties. In this sense, AI has also been demonstrated to be effective in analyzing and predicting the success of the outcome and how it would affect each of the parties in the future (Melzer, 2018). In addition, AI provides accurate, easy-to-use and efficient translation services that reduce miscommunications and other language barriers, making international communication much more fluent, straightforward and efficient. The implementation of these services has been demonstrated to reduce the distance between countries by over 35% (Melzer, 2018).

Third, AI supports international expansion by automating routine tasks therefore increasing productivity and efficiency. This supports international companies in focusing on relevant value-added activities that would boost business innovation in the future and therefore the competitive advantage of the firm (Tidd & Bessant, 2020). In this sense, AI systems are supporting and even replacing low-level repetitive activities, such as for example bureaucratic and other exports and/or tariffs related administrative routines. Benefits in this context include (i) a reduction of the likelihood of errors and delays, (ii) promotion of efficiency, reducing frustration, and therefore enhancing motivation of the workforce, and (iii) support to workers in focusing on value added activities, contributing to the overall value creation of the company in a more efficient way.

Fourth, AI alongside other technologies such as cloud computing, Internet of Things or Big Data, has great implications for knowledge management exchange. Advanced technologies store and ensure easy access to data, provide real time status of objects, and help service platforms to coordinate activities among regions (Alan et al., 2022). In addition, it improves the information shared with international partners, contributing to international negotiations (see above) and therefore to a better selection of partners and a better communication within and between companies.

But the greater effect of AI in the international business context is in the management of the global supply chain. AI facilitates the management of global and complex production units, including warehouse, as it improves demand prediction. This supports a better alignment between manufacturing and delivering functions, enhancing, therefore, the efficiency of the entire value chain. Furthermore, the use of robots is expected to contribute to increase the speed and accuracy in functions such as packing and assembling. Working alongside humans, the use of robots reduces the risk of injuries in dangerous environments in the manufacturing line (Deloitte, 2022). Finally, AI has an impact in smart manufacturing, aligning digital and physical processes within companies and across functions in the supply chain to optimize supply and demand requirements using internet-connected systems (Qu et al., 2019). This considers simple equipment, machines and self-maintenance at the factory level, more efficient communications between functions and other companies along the supply chain, and a better ability to produce just-in-time tailor-made customers' specifications. Cost efficiency due to logistics efficiency, optimization of productivity gains, and other saving through the value chain, such as lower transportation and eventually labor costs, are therefore major benefits of AI.

5.4 Challenges and the Future of AI in the International Business Environment

Covid-19 and its effects have had a disruptive impact on global supply (Khan et al., 2022). As a result of the global disruption, companies have been trying to relocate some of their international activities and boost domestic production. So it is in this context that AI would play an important role. The post-pandemic world is demanding a greater customization of products, increasingly delivered online. In addition, supply chains need to be more resilient and also need to be able to better estimate demand, improving production and distribution capabilities. Firms are looking to diversify localization, targeting closer regions, maintaining productivity, while relying less on large global supply chains (see "friend-shoring" in Chapter 3). In this context, AI, and robotics in particular, will be of great benefit for companies in their decisions of relocating manufacturing activities to their home countries. Also 3D printers could contribute to and create shorter and more local value chains (Alan et al., 2022).

In any case, AI is still a relatively new technology and its real impact in international business and economics is developing gradually and will be evident only in the medium term (Bughin et al., 2018). In the short term, several challenges are arising. On the one hand, the gap between countries, companies, and workers may widen as a consequence of an uneven implementation and the different rates of adoption among industries and markets. AI can deliver a boost to economic activities, but the distribution of benefits is likely to be unbalanced (Yogesh et al., 2021). Rule-based and repetitive manufacturing tasks will highly likely being replaced, displacing jobs within developing counties and emerging markets (Yogesh et al., 2021), broadening therefore the gap between regions. On the other hand, the disruption that comes with AI can lead to some firms not adapting or not adopting the new technology, leaving the market and therefore workers losing jobs or forced to transition to new ones. In this sense, it seems necessary for institutions and companies to develop the necessary frameworks and support to refresh skills, knowledge, and abilities of the workforce, so resources could be redeployed to more productive parts of the economy.

Also, trade rules and regulations must be updated and adapted to the AI new reality, so at the same time a balanced development, access, and use of AI in the international context is ensured. Data management and AI are intertwined, and providing global access to data is expected to support the development of AI systems able to respond to the diverse challenges and to different groups of populations, especially in small and developing countries where restrictions on global data are having a greater impact (Verbeke & Lee, 2022). Some agreements in this context have already been achieved, as for example in the Comprehensive and Progressive Agreement for Trans-Pacific Partnership (CPTPP) and, more recently, in the United States-Mexico-Canada Agreement (USMCA) which includes the commitment to support the development of and access to AI. Similarly, the need to regulate at international level on GDPR, the privacy of data and intellectual property seems to be a must. The key challenge in this area would be to design privacy rules that do not create unnecessary restrictions on access to and use of data. Trade rules can assist by, for example, including commitments of data-importing nations to protect the privacy of personal data from data-exporting countries (Melzer, 2018).

Finally, the future of AI seems to be shaped by the race undertaken by China and the US to win the technological competition. The US is developing large investments in AI and underlying technologies to slow China's plans to reach the technological edge, in addition to further specific measures against the country as defined by President Joe Biden. The last one was imposed in October 2022, when the US government decided to introduce restrictions to exports of chips, software, and other equipment to China needed to produce semiconductors and slow its progress in the development of AI (Financial Times Reporters, 2022). The American president is also stopping American firms from investing in Chinese tech companies and further restrictions are expected to come in 2023. For its part, China has decided to continue pushing its tech industry to move the country towards technological self-sufficiency, especially in the context of AI. Chinese companies benefit from strong support from the government and will receive big incentives to continue engaging in research and development and to continue developing the "new industrial revolution" in the words of President Xi Jinping (Weinland, 2022). However, with China's growing isolation due to an increasing inward-looking focus of the latest policies and the Covid-zero strategy, the positive outlook of the Chinese government seems not to be that clear anymore. International talent and cooperation have been crucial for the impressive development of China in the field of innovation and would still be key for the country's present and future competitiveness (The Economist reporters, 2022). What seems a reality is that this situation between the two largest economies will accelerate their gradual decoupling and a more than probable division of the global economy and business environment into two blocks.

5.5   Application and Discussion

AI is a key piece of how platforms work (see Chapter 4). For example, in Netflix, AI creates a set of recommendations along with a personalized experience that help members to discover relevant content which as a consequence generate engagement and prevent abandonment. This has proved much stronger than traditional methods to present content like listings with sort and filter functionalities or most popular/top-rated non-personalized recommendations; Netflix has a retention rate of 93% compared to Hulu's 64% and Amazon Prime's 75%. Netflix's AI can also customize the trailer and movie/series promotional poster based on the user's profile and history; in fact about 75% of its user activity is based on personalized recommendations and the recommendation system accounts for about 80% of the content streamed (Kapoor, 2021). If a user is a fan of romantic movies/series, then Netflix's AI can show a romantic scene in, for example, an adventure movie; the same movie is also advertised differently to other users based on their preferences and history. Figure 5.1 presents an example of personalization based on genre. Additionally, using Machine Learning, Netflix predicts what a subscriber is most likely

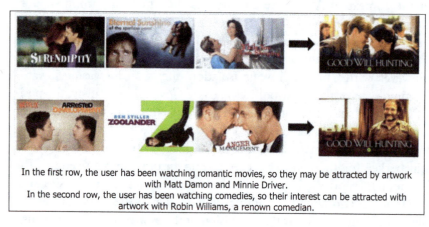

In the first row, the user has been watching romantic movies, so they may be attracted by artwork with Matt Damon and Minnie Driver.
In the second row, the user has been watching comedies, so their interest can be attracted with artwork with Robin Williams, a renown comedian.

Fig. 5.1   Example of personalization based on genre. (Adapted from Kapoor, 2021)

to play and preloads the highly predicted video, reducing thus the load-ing time when a user clicks on that video.

In this context, an important part of the global success of South Korea's Squid Game[1] is a result of Netflix's AI. Mainly due to the recommenda-tions from the platform, Squid Game became the most-watched series on Netflix (in both English and non-English), and also the top one in 94 countries (including the US and UK), with more than 142 million mem-ber households, and around 1.65 billion viewing hours during its first four weeks from launch (surpassing Bridgerton by 2.6 times, the previ-ously most-watched series) (Spangler, 2021). This is a major milestone in the consumption of content from non-mainstream and non-English con-tent. To support the recommendations from AI, the Netflix platform pro-vided access to 200+ million homes around the world, dubbed versions in 34 languages, and subtitles in 37 languages; these, along with stream-ing's lack of time-and-space constraints, expanded the potential custom-ers for local language series/movies. The combination of customized recommendations and making international content widely available and easy to watch has reduced drastically the entry barriers and helped to discover different stories for more people.

Squid Game is considered part of the "Korean Wave", the increase of global popularity of South Korean culture and media since the 2000s, along with the pop band BTS or the 2019 Academy Award Winning movie Parasite. But what is worth noting is that nothing of the scale reached by Squid Game has ever come from anywhere but Hollywood, which supports the argument made earlier on the role of digitalization and technology in helping non-incumbent firms to reach different and diverse markets and as a consequence exponential growth. In fact, "opera-tors of other streaming services with original content, such as Disney+, Paramount+ and Apple TV+, have begun looking to follow Netflix's model of discovering regional content beyond Hollywood and finding similarly successful works for their platforms" (Vourlias, 2021). Figure 5.2 presents the most popular Non-English TV series on Netflix; it can be seen that along with South Korea's "Squid Game", "Extraordinary Attorney Woo", and "All of us are dead", "Money Heist" and "Elite" from

---

[1] https://www.netflix.com/es-en/title/81040344

Most Popular TV (Non-English)

The Top 10 most popular TV (Non-English), based
on hours viewed in their first 28 days on Netflix.

#	TV (Non-English) ⌄	HOURS VIEWED IN FIRST 28 DAYS
1	Squid Game: Season 1	1,650,450,000
2	Money Heist: Part 5	792,230,000
3	Money Heist: Part 4	619,010,000
4	All of Us Are Dead: Season 1	560,780,000
5	Money Heist: Part 3	426,400,000
6	Extraordinary Attorney Woo: Season 1	402,470,000
7	Café con aroma de mujer: Season 1	326,910,000
8	Lupin: Part 1	316,830,000
9	Elite: Season 3	275,300,000
10	Who Killed Sara?: Season 1	266,430,000

Fig. 5.2 Most popular Non-English TV series on Netflix. (Adapted from Netflix, 2022)

Spain, "Who killed Sara?" from Mexico, or "Café con aroma de mujer" from Colombia have conquered audiences beyond their original markets due mainly to the reach of platforms and within this their AI-led recommendations.

Another example of the use of AI in an international context is Mercado Libre [2], the leading e-commerce marketplace founded in Argentina with around 200 million active users in 18 countries in Latin America. The company relies on AI to provide a better and personalized customer experience across its markets in the following areas:

• Understand the customer to reduce the contact time. Through a Machine Learning model using Natural Language Process, they identify problems from consumers' texts, classify the customers, and link them with the most suitable service agent (without the need of further questioning).

---

[2] https://mercadolibre.com/

- Infer users' feelings. Through a model based on Natural Language Process, AI infers the attitude of consumers contacting customer service (angry, frustrated, neutral, or happy) and informs/prevents the agents to treat them accordingly (and eventually offer compensation).
- Predict the need to provide service to customers. Through forecasting based on AI, the company can make decisions on the availability of agents to provide a faster service to consumers.
- Image analysis. Customers send pictures of problems with packages or products, the AI model identifies and classifies them and provides the relevant information (order number, supplier, address, dates, etc) to the service agents to offer a quick and efficient response.

A third example of how AI is supporting companies to grow is its use in intelligent paywalls to drive subscriptions. For several years paywalls have been clumsy and porous, with little knowledge of what was driving conversions. However, as the data improved, it became possible to improve the predictability of a casual browser converting into a subscriber, or the propensity to subscribe. This development is key for business models based on recurring revenues, operating in diverse international markets, where subscriptions are business critical.

This solution is being used by the Wall Street Journal [3]. Through AI, non-subscribed visitors to wsj.com get a score that indicates the propensity score (basically a unique subscription probability) which is the result of 60+ variables like the number and frequency of visits (or if it is the first time), recency, depth, preferred content types, the operating system, the type of device, or the location (and the demographic information that comes with it). Non-subscribed visitors are categorized as hot, warm, or cold. Those with propensity scores higher than a certain level (indicating a higher probability of subscribing) will hit a hard paywall (i.e., requiring a paid subscription before providing access to any content). Those with lower propensity scores are offered free access to the site for one session before the paywall. Or they are offered guest access to the site in various time increments, in exchange for providing an email address (to get more

---

[3] www.WSJ.com

variables to analyze). Guest access is also offered based on a visitor's score, aimed at people whose scores indicate they could be persuaded into subscribing if tempted with a little more content (Wang, 2018).

5.6   Concluding Remarks

Following on from previous chapters, technology is changing the way international business is conducted and more importantly it is opening new opportunities for companies to operate in diverse and distant environments. Within this, AI has been increasingly included in the operations of business over the last 15+ years for routine administrative processes, cost reduction, management of supply chains, or manufacturing automation. It is also increasingly being used to improve and personalize the customer experience, and as a consequence to increase revenues.

In this context, this chapter has discussed and analyzed the impact of AI in international business, showing how diverse activities and industries like logistics, transportation, financial and professional services, marketing and advertisement, agriculture, or health care are being changed by the use of AI. This is having big impacts in the labor market and job opportunities, with an expected increase in the demand for skilled technological profiles with more creative and cognitive orientated roles in support of AI technologies.

Within this, a key development is the possibility to provide personalized offers to customers and even modify their consumer behavior. Squid Game, the South Korean series available in Netflix, is a good example of this. Through personalized recommendations from AI and the wide reach of the platform, it has become the most-watched series on Netflix in both English and non-English, marking a milestone for non-English content and also showing the degree of influence of personalized recommendations in the consumption patterns in different markets (even in those used to consum more mainstream content in English).

AI is expected to be a major contributor to global growth, with some estimates reaching up to 26% of global GCP by 2030 (Bughin et al., 2018). This is because it increases the productivity, facilitates cross-cultural communication (and as a consequence international negotiations), enables knowledge management exchange, and improves the management of global supply chains. For international business AI helps to reduce the liability of foreignness by improving communication and also by deepening the understanding of the consumption patterns of overseas consumers. Also, in combination with platforms, it helps to internalize the transaction costs as seen in the examples of Mercado Libre and paywalls.

Having said this, AI's real impact in international business is developing gradually and will be evident only in the medium term. In the short term, a major challenge is the widening gap in the adoption and implementation of AI among countries, companies, and workers; gaps that can bring unbalanced benefits. Trade rules and regulations need to be adapted to a context increasingly influenced by AI; they need to incorporate/recognize the privacy and intellectual property of data, for example including commitments of data-importing nations to protect the privacy of personal data from the data-exporting country (Meltzer, 2018).

References

Accenture Research. (2021). *The art of AI maturity. Advancing from practice to performance*. Retrieved from https://www.accenture.com/us-en/insights/artificial-intelligence/ai-maturity-and-transformation.

Alan, A. A., Noemi, S., Yelnur, S., Rudolf, R. S., & Nikolay, M. (2022). Advanced technologies and international business: A multidisciplinary analysis of the literature. *International Business Review, 31*(4), 101967. https://doi.org/10.1016/j.ibusrev.2021.101967

Andrea, S., & Andrea De, M. (2021). Leveraging artificial intelligence in business: Implications, applications and methods. *Technology Analysis & Strategic Management, 34*(1), 16–29. https://doi.org/10.1080/09537325.2021.1883583

Balakrishnan, T., Chui, M., & Henke, N. (2020). *The state of AI in 2020*. Retrieved from https://www.mckinsey.com/capabilities/quantumblack/our-insights/global-survey-the-state-of-ai-in-2020

Brynjolfsson, E., Hui, X., & Liu, M. (2019). Does machine translation affect international trade? Evidence from a large digital platform. *Management Science, 65*(12), 5449–5460. https://doi.org/10.1287/mnsc.2019.3388

Bughin, J., Seong, J., Manyika, J., Chui, M., & Joshi, R. (2018). *Notes from the AI frontier modeling the impact of AI on the world economy.* Mckinsey Global Institute. Retrieved from https://www.mckinsey.com/~/media/McKinsey/Featured%20Insights/Artificial%20Intelligence/Notes%20from%20the%20frontier%20Modeling%20the%20impact%20of%20AI%20on%20the%20world%20economy/MGI-Notes-from-the-AI-frontier-Modeling-the-impact-of-AI-on-the-world-economy-September-2018.ashx

Chappell, J. (2020). *Artificial Intelligence: From predictive to prescriptive and beyond.* Retrieved from https://insource.solutions/wp-content/uploads/2020/05/WhitePaper_AIfromPredictivetoPrescriptiveandBeyond-EN.pdf

Deloitte. (2022). *Using autonomous robots to drive supply chain innovation.* Retrieved from https://www2.deloitte.com/us/en/pages/manufacturing/articles/autonomous-robots-supply-chain-innovation.html

Ferencz, J., López-González, J., & Oliván, I. (2022). Artifical intelligence and international trade. Some preliminary implications. *OECD Trade Policy, 260.* Retrieved from https://www.oecd-ilibrary.org/docserver/13212d3e-en.pdf?expires=1667908068&id=id&accname=guest&checksum=9015F2532974C3E24F619FA3A636AA81

Financial Times Reporters. (2022). How the US chip export controls have turned the screws on China. *Financial Times.* Retrieved from https://www.ft.com/content/bbbdc7dc-0566-4a05-a7b3-27afd82580f3.

Kapoor, V. (2021, 23 July 2021). How Netflix uses big data for consumer satisfaction. *The Economic Tribune.* Retrieved from https://www.econtribune.com/post/how-netflix-uses-big-data-for-customer-satisfaction

Khan, S. A. R., Piprani, A. Z., & Yu, Z. (2022). Supply chain analytics and post-pandemic performance: mediating role of triple-A supply chain strategies. *International Journal of Emerging Markets,* ahead-of-print(ahead-of-print). doi:https://doi.org/10.1108/IJOEM-11-2021-1744.

Loureiro, S., Guerreiro, J., & Iis, T. (2021). Artificial intelligence in business: State of the art and future research agenda. *Journal of Business Research, 129,* 911–926. https://doi.org/10.1016/j.jbusres.2020.11.001

Marr, B. (2022). What is the impact of Artificial Intelligence (AI) On Society? Retrieved from https://bernardmarr.com/what-is-the-impact-of-artificial-intelligence-ai-on-society/#:~:text=Artificial%20intelligence%20can%20dramatically%20improve,creativity%20and%20empathy%20among%20others.

Meltzer, J. (2018, 13 December 2018). The impact of artificial intelligence on international trade. *Brookings*. Retrieved from https://www.brookings.edu/research/the-impact-of-artificial-intelligence-on-international-trade/.

Melzer, J. (2018). *The impact of artificial intelligence on international trade.* Retrieved from https://www.brookings.edu/research/the-impact-of-artificial-intelligence-on-international-trade/

Netflix. (2022). Most Popular TV (Non-English). Retrieved from https://top10.netflix.com/tv-non-english

Neufeld, D. (2021). Long Waves: The History of Innovation Cycles. Retrieved from https://www.visualcapitalist.com/the-history-of-innovation-cycles/

Qu, Y. J., Ming, X. G., Liu, Z. W., Zhang, X. Y., & Hou, Z. T. (2019). Smart manufacturing systems: State of the art and future trends. *The International Journal of Advanced Manufacturing Technology, 103*(9), 3751–3768. https://doi.org/10.1007/s00170-019-03754-7

Ruiz-Real, J. L., Uribe-Toril, J., Torres, J. A., & De Pablo, J. (2021). Artificial intelligence in business and economics research: Trends and future. *Journal of Business Economics and Management, 22*(1), 98–117. https://doi.org/10.3846/jbem.2020.13641

Scoglio, A. A., Reilly, E. D., Gorman, J. A., & Drebing, C. E. (2019). Use of social robots in mental health and well-being research: Systematic review. *Journal of Medical Internet Research, 21*(7), e13322. https://doi.org/10.2196/13322

Spangler, T. (2021, 16 November 2021). 'Squid Game' Is Decisively Netflix No. 1 Show of All Time With 1.65 Billion Hours Streamed in First Four Weeks, Company Says. *Variety*. Retrieved from https://variety.com/2021/digital/news/squid-game-all-time-most-popular-show-netflix-1235113196/

The Economist reporters. (2022, 13/10/2022). China and the West are in a race to foster innovation. *The Economist*.

Tidd, J., & Bessant, J. (2020). *Managing innovation: Integrating technological, market and organizational change* (7th ed.). Wiley.

Verbeke, A., & Lee, I. (2022). *International business strategy. Rethinking the foundations of global corporate success* (3rd ed.). Cambridge University Press.

Vourlias, C. (2021, 18 October 2021). In the Hunt for the Next 'Squid Game,' Industry Execs See 'Unlimited Potential'. *Variety*. Retrieved from https://variety.com/2021/streaming/global/squid-game-netflix-paramount-plus-global-hits-1235091468/

Wang, S. (2018). After years of testing, The Wall Street Journal has built a paywall that bends to the individual reader. Retrieved from https://www. niemanlab.org/2018/02/after-years-of-testing-the-wall-street-journal-has-built-a-paywall-that-bends-to-the-individual-reader/

Weinland, D. (2022, 18/11/2022). The tech war between America and China is just getting started. *The Economist.*

Yogesh, K. D., Laurie, H., Elvira, I., Gert, A., Crispin, C., Tom, C., et al. (2021). Artificial intelligence (AI): Multidisciplinary perspectives on emerging challenges, opportunities, and agenda for research, practice and policy. *International Journal of Information Management, 57,* 101994. https://doi.org/10.1016/j.ijinfomgt.2019.08.002

6

Data Management and Regulations for International Business

Abstract Data flows have become a strategic asset for companies as they allow for coordination and optimization of the global value chain, a more efficient access to global customers, or the automation of processes leading to reduction of costs. In a business context in which the use of data is increasing exponentially, the main concern today relates to how and where data are collected, transferred, and used, and to what extent privacy, at both private and national levels, is secured. It is in this context that the chapter provides a critical discussion of the current regulatory framework for data management across borders and assesses the future needs in the field. Despite the three common global frameworks (US, EU, and China), there are still different approaches at regional and national levels reflecting cultural differences and diverse national interests. The analysis shows that a holistic, comprehensive, and coherent system could be implemented for the digital economy led and coordinated by international organizations in cooperation with governments, policy makers, companies, and individuals. However, politics and geopolitics are taking precedence over business, economics, and technology development. This fragmentation represents the main challenge for the different

© The Author(s), under exclusive license to Springer Nature Switzerland AG 2023
G. Fornes, M. Altamira, *Digitalization, Technology and Global Business*,
https://doi.org/10.1007/978-3-031-33111-4_6

stakeholders involved in the digital economy engaging with new technologies.

Keywords Data regulations • International data management • Data legal frameworks • Digital sovereignty • Splinternet

> *"To me the biggest question for the future is will we really continue in the future to license spectrum—do governments license oxygen? No. The Internet is oxygen, it's water."*
> —Vittorio Colao, Chief Executive Officer, Vodafone Group, United Kingdom, *(Colao, 2015)*

6.1   Introduction

As a result of the increasing adoption of new digital business models, firms from all industries and sizes are exposed to data in their everyday operations. From a global perspective, it seems impossible to think of a single transaction not requiring cross-border data transfers (Casalini & Lopez Gonzalez, 2019). It is in this context that data flows have become a strategic asset for companies. Digital data allows for coordination and optimization of the global value chain, a more efficient access to global customers, or the automation of processes leading to reduction of costs. In addition, data provides the information needed for other economic activities to be developed in an efficient and timely manner and even data itself can be the object of transaction as it is in the case of trade in services. In other words, data management has become a key capability supporting companies in reaching their strategic goals, being the essence of today's international business and trade relations (Daza Jaller et al., 2020).

In this context, there is a need to understand how data works, the value of data, and more importantly, how/if the use of data can be regulated to ensure a fair use across borders to support the development of new technologies as well as the sustainable growth of new digital data-driven business models (Ahmed, 2019). Data flows are a relatively novel phenomenon, meaning that its exchange across borders has given rise to concerns for citizens, companies, governments and policymakers. The main concern is related to how and where data are collected, transferred, and used, and to what extent privacy, at both private (individuals and companies) and national levels, is secured when doing cross-border transactions (Casalini & Lopez Gonzalez, 2019). This represents a complex scenario which has become even more challenging by the fact that different countries around the globe have set up different regulatory frameworks with diverse scopes, scales, and approaches to implementation. As a result, global institutions are in the process of updating and defining new data management regulations.

An international data management framework that enables sound and solid foundations of digital markets across the globe is a necessity in order to support global and sustainable growth through innovation (Fink, 2020). In this context, the present chapter provides a critical discussion of the current regulatory framework for data management across borders, and of the present and future challenges. An application and discussion section with real cases from the business environment is included at the end.

6.2   Data Flows and Regulations. Directions Towards Global Rulemaking?

There are three main regulatory frameworks about personal data flows treatment, data protection and privacy, and data management. The model developed in the United States (US), the model applied in the European Union (EU), and the model implemented in China. The three models reflect the main institutional structures and economic realities of the three main trading blocks and lead to very different business and economic outlooks. On the one hand, the framework applied by the US considers an open approach to local data transfers and processing with a baseline setting privacy principles and companies having the flexibility and responsibility to self-regulate cross-border data transfers.

On the other hand, the EU model is based on conditional local data transfers, giving priority to the protection of personal data rights in the Union through the General Data Protection Regulation (GDPR). This regulation requires consent for data collection and processing along with very specific conditions to access, modify, or delete data. In the case of cross-border data transfers, several requirements also apply, for example the consent of the data subject or the use of binding corporate rules. This model is followed by many countries outside the EU, being the framework that covers the biggest portion of global digital business and trade (Van der Marel, 2021).

Finally, China has defined a regulatory framework characterized by strong controls of data processing and transfers where data are considered a matter of national security, usually linked to cybersecurity (Van der Marel, 2021). Within this context and under the premise of security and protection of personal data, China's cross-border data flows policies are seeking the definition of international coordination rules as well as free and trustable data transmission processes through government-led initiatives such as the "Global Initiative on Data Security" and the "Global Security Initiative" (Chin & Zhao, 2022).

These three models reflect three different economic realities and have different impacts in the business environment. First, a more free and flexible data management model at domestic level is said to encourage innovation and may lead to a boost in productivity in the US. Second, the regulatory structure in the EU and China is said to restrict digital innovation as a driver of growth, with less focus on radical technological innovation but with emphasis on developing goods and services with technologies already tested. In the case of China, the particularities of the environment can lead to state-led innovations following the goals and policies of the Chinese government, as reflected in its regulatory framework (Chin & Zhao, 2022; Van der Marel, 2021).

However, and despite the three dominant models setting the basis for data management in around 65% of the world's economy (Van der Marel, 2021), the reality is that different regions and countries have adopted different approaches. This means that today's digital economy and business environment operate within a rather fragmented and incomplete framework at multilateral, regional, and bilateral levels. For this reason, companies, governments, and policymakers are trying to reduce the gaps to facilitate international digital trade while balancing each party's interests (Lippoldt, 2022). In this context, and in order to understand the current situation, the global regulatory framework of data management can be divided into three main levels regarding the definition of rules and their application (Casalini & Lopez Gonzalez, 2019): (i) domestic data regulation with cross-border elements; ii) international data protection instruments developed by international institutions; and iii) data-flows considerations in international trade agreements.

(i) Domestic data regulations with cross-border elements

At the present time, data-driven business models are becoming increasingly relevant to the development of the economy; governments and policy makers are adapting domestic legislations to the digital ecosystem. This is creating a very heterogenous international scenario in which each country develops its own regulatory system regarding (i) cross-border data transfers but with different levels of freedom of flows, and (ii) diverse requirements for local storage of data depending on national interests. In addition, these regulations vary across sectors, industries and types of firms depending on the country, creating a challenging situation for companies operating internationally.

(ii) International data protection instruments developed by international institutions

In order to address and face the challenges of the very diverse domestic regulations, several instruments to ensure the protection of privacy and a fair and reliable access to data across countries have been defined by international institutions. This is the case with the OECD Privacy Guidelines that provide formal recommendations on issues such as Electronic Authentication, Consumer Protection in E-Commerce (2016), or Enhancing Access to and Sharing of Data (OECD, 2013). In 2021, negotiations among OECD and the G20 members resulted in 136 rules on the taxation of cross-border digital services that will enter into force in 2023.

Also, The Convention for the Protection of Individuals with regard to Automatic Processing of Personal Data, and The APEC Cross-Border Privacy Rules (CBPR) System promote recommendations for the management of data at global level (European Parliament XE "European Parliament" , 2020). Furthermore, the United Nations (UN) has developed a variety of frameworks, such as the legal tool Model Law on Electronic Commerce or the UN Economic Commission for Europe (UNECE), to support global rulemaking focused on cybersecurity. The UNCTAD has also developed a monitoring framework to create awareness on e-commerce good practices while providing policy recommendations and digital trade statistics (Lippoldt, 2022). Regarding AI and its significant impact on the economy and society, the World Intellectual Property Organization (WIPO) is currently developing guidelines and preliminary considerations for its Member States and other stakeholders to regulate the application of AI with regards intellectual property (Alvarez-Risco & Del-Aguila-Arcentales, 2021).

Moreover, in 2021, the Group of Seven (G7) trade ministers issued a set of digital trade principles with the main goal of consolidating and homogenizing elements from digital trade and data management for its members creating open digital markets with free, trustable data flows (i.e., with data protection). This includes a safe digital environment for workers, consumers, and businesses, digital government services, and a fair and inclusive global governance engaging the World Trade Organization (WTO), the OECD, and the World Customs Organization (Lippoldt, 2022).

Indeed, one of the most active institutions in global rulemaking is the World Trade Organization (WTO) (European Parliament, 2020; Meltzer, 2019). The WTO provides a multilateral trade negotiations environment for its members and is the most suitable venue to negotiate and resolve disputes regarding cross-border data flows issues. In fact, the WTO set up in 1998 a working group on e-commerce to deal with trade-related intellectual property rights while promoting responsive changes in digital trade (Chin & Zhao, 2022). A major policy defined by the WTO in recent years is the General Agreement on Trade in Services (GATS), the first multilateral agreement for the liberalization of international trade in services that eliminates trade barriers for all services except for those provided by governments (WTO, 2013). Also, the WTO Facilitation Agreement is enhancing the digitalization of some customs processes, as well as improving transparency in trade relations (WTO, 2017). However, its progress over the past 20 years has been slow, and the multilateral regulatory framework available today is still inconsistent and incomplete mainly due to cultural differences and very diverse national interests on the matter. In 2019, 71 members signed a joint statement to commence negotiations on trade-related aspects of e-commerce (WTO, 2019).

To close the gaps, policy makers in leading economies are focusing their attention on regional and bilateral trade agreements for the flows of data and data management.

(iii) The treatment of dataflows in international trade agreements

Despite the differences of the three dominant regulatory models mentioned above, recent regional trade agreements have demonstrated a certain degree of overlap and they are increasingly incorporating chapters on cross-border data flows to fill the gaps of incomplete international frameworks. Examples include the Canada European Union Comprehensive Economic and Trade Agreement (CETA) which defines provisions related to copyrights, a level playing field for intellectual property, and regulations on electronic services. Other examples are the Comprehensive and Progressive Trans-Pacific Partnership (CPTPP) or the United States-Mexico-Canada Agreement (USMCA) USMCA; in both cases free flows of data are encouraged with some personal data protection clauses. Also, in the context of developing countries, the Regional Comprehensive Economic Partnership (RCEP) has been dealing with data protection rules in a more flexible manner, providing differential treatments depending on the level of industrial and economic development of the country (Chin & Zhao, 2022). Finally, third counties also have their own bilateral agreements setting their own standards for data exchange-related issues, as is the case regarding Japan with the EU or the US with Australia.

All in all, it is evident that new data flows defining the current business environment require new regulatory models, the challenge being how to find a common approach to facilitate a more homogenous scenario (Meltzer, 2019). As (Chin & Zhao, 2022) suggest, a more focused and concrete scope of the WTO agreement on e-commerce rules and on cross-border data flows with sufficient room to cater for each members' interests regarding security, stability, and privacy would be a key next step.

To do this, the perceived risks and threats of consumers and businesses need be considered. A study from the OECD (Casalini & Lopez Gonzalez, 2019) highlighted the major concerns of consumers to be how personal data are being treated, the risks regarding a wrong use of data, or the theft of information. Companies were also concerned about keeping data safe, about guaranteeing trust when operating online through digital platforms, as well as about the impact of the heterogeneous emerging data measures on the costs and the management of global value chains. They were also worried about the impact that this fragmented framework has when engaging in trade with companies abroad. Failure to understand the different stakeholders' needs and challenges and therefore to achieve a common framework will further fragment digital trade and services. It will also impact negatively the development of new technologies and the growth of the digital economy around the globe (Ahmed, 2019).

International business and trade rules should therefore seek to define sound regulatory solutions to provide the necessary tools, guarantees, and trust for citizens, companies and governments that are increasingly involved in international business and trade as a consequence of digitalization and the use and management of data. New initiatives towards this direction have recently been announced by Brussels for the European context. On the one hand, the Digital Services Act agreed between EU member states, the European Commission and the European Parliament, in a legislative package setting for the first time, provides rules for big technological companies to comply with in order to improve and guarantee online users' safety, with special attention to minors. The act also addresses issues such as misinformation or propaganda (Espinoza, 2022b). On the other hand, the Digital Markets Acts, expected to be applicable from beginning of 2023, has the goal of ensuring fair and trustworthy behavior of big digital platforms (Espinoza, 2022a; European Commission, 2022). Both initiatives are key elements of the European digital strategy of the European Commission, intended to address the opportunities and challenges of digital transformation in the post-Covid era.

6.3   Application and Discussion

A sound and clear international framework for the transfer and management of data is needed to seize the major opportunities that digital economy and technology are bringing to business in particular and to societies in general. This especially affects new technologies, such as AI, which are expected to create drastic changes in the near future. In addition to the extra barriers and costs that a fragmented framework brings, AI models run on large datasets, and having these datasets fragmented due to different regulations will delay new developments. Or even worst, the results will perpetuate the bias as machines will learn from the data available within their framework.

For example, Artificial Intelligence (AI) and Machine Learning (ML) models are being applied in the development of new drugs which is proving to reduce the risks of different stages of this process. In the discovery phase, an AI algorithm may predict the safety profile of the new drug on the basis of the characteristics of its therapeutic target and molecular interactions (Yin et al., 2021). In the pre-clinical phase, a computational alignment between the molecular profile of preclinical tumor models and actual patient tumor samples may inform on the translatability of the preclinical findings into clinical effects (Trastulla et al., 2022). In the clinical phase, AI/ML systems may help identify molecular patterns associated with drug response versus resistance through integrated analysis of multi-omics data from patient samples (Cai et al., 2022).

But the barriers and fragmentation of data are creating bias in the outputs. For example, a study on medical imaging found a decrease in performance for underrepresented genders when a minimum gender balance was not fulfilled (Larrazabal et al., 2020). Another study on the diagnosis of melanoma (a tumor which is responsible for the majority of skin cancer-associated deaths) showed that, as most ML models are trained on samples of patients with fair skin color, they underperform on images of lesions of patients with a darker skin color (Adamson & Smith, 2018). It will be a waste of opportunities that the current biases in gender or race are maintained due to barriers to access data.

The examples above are technical issues related to the population (*N*) on which results are inferred, or in other words whether *N=all* or it is a sample (*n*) biased by the data generated, available, and stored (Harford, 2014). But the underlying issue seems to be the dominance of digital sovereignty, the control of data, software, standards, and protocols to complement the traditional analogue sovereignty (the control of territory, resources, and people) (Floridi, 2020). As a consequence, "technology wars are becoming the new trade wars" (Garcia-Macia & Goyal, 2021).

The source is that the interconnections of the digital age have blurred the distinctions between economic and security issues where dominant tech companies are both engines of economic growth and channels of security risks. Therefore, trade and industrial policies can be hijacked by broader security and geopolitical priorities. As a consequence, the so-called "splinternet" is breaking the online world "into competing digital spheres, partly thanks to three incompatible models of handling data—European privacy-focused regulation, US corporate-driven free-for-all, and Chinese state surveillance" (Thornhill, 2021).

The increase in digital trade restrictions is presented in Fig. 6.1. It can be seen that since 2015 most countries have been tightening their digital trade policies. This reverses the trend seen with goods and services over the last 20 to 30 years (see Chap. 1). This is because, different from traditional goods and services where barriers to trade usually lower economic outputs, leadership in digital markets brings the possibility to set standards and therefore dominate global markets. New technologies like AI, IoT, or quantum computing are new sources of growth expected to transform industries and increase productivity (Garcia-Macia & Goyal, 2021). And because big tech companies rely on economies of scale and scope, a few highly productive and innovative firms are dominating global markets and benefiting from large profits (IMF, 2019).

6.4   Concluding Remarks

The aim of this chapter has been to provide an overview of the different approaches to global data management rulemaking to understand the challenges and future needs in the field. The analysis revealed that despite

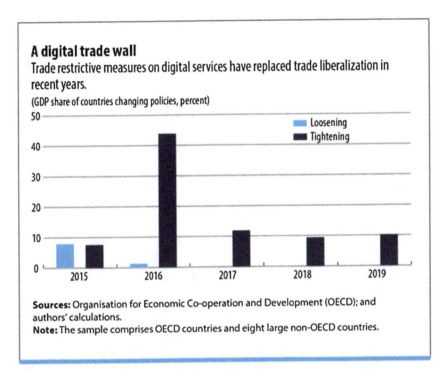

Fig. 6.1 Digital trade restrictions. (Adapted from Garcia-Macia & Goyal, 2021)

the three common global frameworks (US, EU, and China), there are still different approaches at regional and national levels reflecting cultural differences and diverse national interests. While international organizations are trying to reduce the gaps, there is a need for further guidance to help governments and policy makers to understand the different challenges and concerns from the different stakeholders regarding the digital economy and the adoption of new digital models and technologies.

As recommended by the OECD (Casalini & Lopez Gonzalez, 2019) this could be done through (i) the analysis of the relevant regulatory approaches to leverage the opportunities while reducing the challenges of the digital transformation; (ii) the identification of the strengths, weaknesses, opportunities and necessary adaptations of existing regulatory policy approaches; and (iii) reflection about how digital technologies and models can help resource-constrained governments and regulators to better regulate. A holistic, comprehensive, and coherent system could be implemented for the digital economy, covering digital trade, domestic digital economy activity, and global relevant policies, regulations, and standards. This can be coordinated by new and/or existing international organizations in cooperation with governments, policy makers, companies, and individuals.

However, politics and geopolitics are taking prevalence over business, economics, and technology development. This is because countries are focused on their digital sovereignty to complement their analogue sovereignty. As new technologies will be generating new sources of growth, transformation in industries, and increases in productivity, countries intend to reap the benefits of setting the standards and therefore dominating global markets. As a consequence, three competing digital spheres of data handling are growing: the US, the EU, and China. This is known as "splinternet".

This fragmentation in the regulations on handling of data is already affecting the results of machine learning models as the data feeding them are not representing the whole population. As mentioned above, ML models using medical digital imaging data are acquiring gender and race biases. Diversity is also an issue, as facial recognition [still] works best on white male faces (Colback, 2020). Another example, Scania, the Swedish truck maker, uses a small box that sends diagnostic data—speed, fuel use, engine performance, even driving technique—to the HQ in Europe. These data are used to improve the products, services, and future developments. But in China, where international data transfers are restricted, the company experiences extra costs in local data storage and needs to segregate the information from the rest of its operations (Beattie, 2018).

References

Adamson, A., & Smith, A. (2018). Machine learning and health care disparities in dermatology. *JAMA Dermatology, 154*(11), 1. https://doi.org/10.1001/jamadermatol.2018.2348

Ahmed, U. (2019). The importance of Cross-border regulatory cooperation in an era of digital trade. *World Trade Review, 18*(S1), S99–S120. https://doi.org/10.1017/S1474745618000514

Alvarez-Risco, A., & Del-Aguila-Arcentales, S. (2021). A note on changing regulation in international business: The world intellectual property organization (WIPO) and artificial intelligence. In A. Verbeke, R. van Tulder, E. L. Rose, & Y. Wei (Eds.), *The multiple dimensions of institutional complexity in international business research* (Vol. 15, pp. 363–371). Emerald Publishing Limited.

Beattie, A. (2018). Data protectionism: the growing menace to global business. *Financial Times*. Retrieved from https://www.ft.com/content/6f0f41e4-47de-11e8-8ee8-cae73aab7ccb.

Cai, Z., Poulos, R., Liu, J., & Zhong, Q. (2022). Machine learning for multiomics data integration in cancer. *iScience, 25*(2), 1. https://doi.org/10.1016/j.isci.2022.103798

Casalini, F., & Lopez Gonzalez, J. (2019). Trade and Cross-Border Data Flows. *OECD Trade Policy Papers* (220). doi: 10.1787/18166873.

Chin, Y.-C., & Zhao, J. (2022). Governing Cross-border data flows: International trade agreements and their limits. *Laws, 11*(4), 63. Retrieved from https://www.mdpi.com/2075-471X/11/4/63

Colao, V. (2015). Speech at the World Economic Forum.

Daza Jaller, L., Gaillard, S., & Molinuevo, M. (2020). The regulation of Digital Trade. Key policies and international trends. In. Washington: World Bank.

Espinoza, J. (2022a). EU to unveil landmark legislation to tackle market power of Big Tech. *Financial Times*. Retrieved from https://www.ft.com/content/1c66027d-717f-4d71-b76b-34077721a678.

Espinoza, J. (2022b). EU to unveil law to force Big Tech to police illegal content. *Financial Times*. Retrieved from https://www.ft.com/content/f39a8b61-c7b4-4674-9606-b923f63ad770.

European Parliament. (2020). *Legal analysis of international trade law and digital trade*. Policy Department for External Relations.

Fink, M. (2020). Legal analysis of international trade law and digital trade. *Think Tank European Parliament*. doi:10.2861/137398.

Floridi, L. (2020). The fight for digital Sovereignity: What it is, and why it matters, especially for the EU. *Philosophy & Technology, 33*, 369–378. https://link.springer.com/article/10.1007/s13347-020-00423-6.

Garcia-Macia, D., & Goyal, R. (2021). Decoupling in the digital era. *Finance & Development. International Monetary Fund*. Retrieved from https://www.imf.org/external/pubs/ft/fandd/2021/03/international-cooperation-and-the-digital-economy-garcia.htm.

Harford, T. (2014, 28 March 2014). Big data: Are we making a big mistake? *Financial Times*.

IMF. (2019). *World economic outlook*. Retrieved from https://www.imf.org/en/Publications/WEO/Issues/2019/03/28/world-economic-outlook-april-2019#Chapter%202

Larrazabal, A., Nieto, N., Peterson, V., Milone, D., & Ferrante, E. (2020). Gender imbalance in medical imaging datasets produces biased classifiers for computer-aided diagnosis. *PNAS, 117*(23), 1. https://www.pnas.org/doi/full/10.1073/pnas.1919012117.

Lippoldt, D. (2022). *Regulating the Digital Economy: Reflections on the Trade and Innovation Nexus*. Paper presented at the Project for Peaceful Competition: Global Cooperation on Digital Governance and the Geoeconomics of New Technologies in a Multi-polar World, Virtual. https://www.cigionline.org/articles/regulating-the-digital-economy-reflections-on-the-trade-and-innovation-nexus/

Meltzer, J. P. (2019). Governing digital trade. *World Trade Review, 18*(S1), S23–S48. https://doi.org/10.1017/S1474745618000502

OECD. (2013). *OECD guidelines on the protection of privacy and transborder flows of personal data*. Retrieved from Paris https://www.oecd.org/sti/ieconomy/oecdguidelinesontheprotectionofprivacyandtransborderflowsofpersonaldata.htm

Trastulla, L., Noorbakhsh, J., Vazquez, F., McFarland, J., & Iorio, F. (2022). Computational estimation of quality and clinical relevance of cancer cell lines. *Molecular Systems Biology, 18*, 1. https://www.embopress.org/doi/full/10.15252/msb.202211017.

Van der Marel, E. (2021). Regulating the globalisation of data: Which model works best? *ECIPE Policy Brief, 9*. Retrieved from https://ecipe.org/wp-content/uploads/2021/05/ECI_21_PolicyBrief_09_2021_LY03.pdf

WTO. (2013). *The general agreement on trade in services*. WTO Trade in Services Division.

WTO. (2019). Joint Initiative on E-commerce [Press release]. Retrieved from https://www.wto.org/english/tratop_e/ecom_e/joint_statement_e.htm

Yin, J., Li, F., Lu, Y., Zeng, S., & Zhu, F. (2021). Identification of the key target profiles underlying the drugs of narrow therapeutic index for treating cancer and cardiovascular disease. *Computational and Structural Biotechnology Journal, 19*, 2318–2328.

7

Conclusions, Challenges, and Trends

Abstract This chapter develops a summary of the main findings of the book and develops some concluding remarks. The book ends with a critical assessment of future challenges and trends. In a context with high uncertainties, new technologies will become mainstream, following the path of AI, and will create a major impact in the economy and also in the possibilities for international expansion of firms. Despite all the challenges discussed in the book, there are still many opportunities to keep increasing living standards across the world through technological developments and economic integration.

Keywords Future of globalization • New technologies • Future trends

"Think of digital transformation less as a technology project to be finished than as a state of perpetual agility, always ready to evolve for whatever customers want next, and you'll be pointed down the right path."
—Amit Zavery, VP and Head of Platform, Google Cloud

© The Author(s), under exclusive license to Springer Nature Switzerland AG 2023
G. Fornes, M. Altamira, *Digitalization, Technology and Global Business*,
https://doi.org/10.1007/978-3-031-33111-4_7

7.1 Recap

The book started by discussing the mainstream concepts and frameworks in International Business and how, as the environment and technology have changed, they have been adapted to keep their explanatory power. What we saw was that the sources of these changes are intertwined, technology has helped to lower barriers to trade, and lower barriers to trade have helped technology to spread quickly. Using the concepts of mainstream theories, the increasing digitalization and globalization (as a result of lowering trade barriers), the main impact has been on:

- Ownership of competitive advantages (O)

  - Probably the one whose impact has changed the least, as without the O advantage it is unlikely that companies could expand (at least in an efficient and sustainable way)
  - Although the nature of firm-specific advantages and capabilities have had to adapt to the new environment
  - And even the definition of MNEs has moved to the idea of digitally networked ecosystems

- Location (L)

  - The focus has moved from physical and territorial attributes, to digital and information flow-based attributes
  - The risk of location has been changing from understanding how host markets work, to identify areas of growth (including low-cost production), and then to minimize [geo]political risk ("friendshoring")

- Internalization of transaction costs (I)

  - They have been reduced greatly
  - There is an increase in network economies, speed, and scalability

- Platforms are helping companies to internalize transactions costs to operate internationally

- Liability of foreignness

  - Its focus has moved to deal with development of relationships, participation in ecosystems, understanding informal institutions, and identifying the sources of competitiveness in host markets
  - Price setting (and the associated knowledge and understanding of host markets) has improved due to technological developments
  - Lower barriers to trade, increasing economic integration among countries, improvements in communication, improvements in transportation, etc are the main reasons for these changes

One of the major beneficiaries of this increase in digitalization and globalization has been the trade of services. The volume of services traded internationally went from very low in the late 80s to almost half of the trade in goods in 2021 (WTO, 2022).

But beyond these self-evident impacts, it has been clear throughout the discussions in the book that digitalization and international expansion still need more research. These are relatively new phenomena and their impact is only now being seen. In fact, it is possible to say that the depth and breadth of the changes and the impact of digitalization, technology, and globalization were realized as a result of the Covid-19-related lockdowns and movement restrictions. The world's economy continued operating thanks to quick changes in work patterns (working from home, for example), to production in [remote] areas with managed lockdowns, or deliveries of everything from everywhere to homes in less than 48 hours in many cases.

In this context, one of the key elements that has supported companies (especially those from non-traditional origins) in their international expansion has been platforms. They have been instrumental in helping to overcome most of the barriers usually associated with internationalization. Platforms are helping companies to minimize the transaction costs of operating internationally and also without the need for firms to internalize these transaction costs. Platforms provide most of the resources needed to serve diverse markets in an efficient way. And more importantly, they allow enterprises to focus on their competitive advantages rather than on also developing new capabilities to operate internationally.

Platforms are vital in reducing the barriers, timeframes, and investments to operate overseas. This reduction in the liability of foreignness has been possible because platforms provide almost direct access to the final consumer regardless of where the producer is located. They also provide a trusted umbrella brand, legal protection, and infrastructure to provide local customer service. And as a consequence of this possibility for exponential growth, platforms have put thousands of companies in the spotlight, most previously unknown to consumers or investors, to receive funding to improve their operations and therefore further reduce the barriers to growth.

Platforms are also changing consumption patterns and as a consequence opening new markets and demand both domestically and internationally. These new opportunities have not all/always been to the detriment of traditional markets; platforms have found new sources of demand for member companies through the use of technology to provide new products/services. They have achieved this by offering more personalized products/services, sharing assets, pricing based on usage, and creating more collaborative ecosystems.

A key technology supporting international operations is AI, which has impacted logistics, transportation, financial and professional services, marketing and advertisement, agriculture, or health care. A major development of AI is the possibility to provide personalized offers to customers and even modify their consumer behavior. AI is expected to maintain a major role in global growth, with some estimates reaching up to 26% of global GCP by 2030 due to increases in productivity, facilitation of cross-cultural communication (and as a consequence, international negotiations), enabling knowledge management exchange, and improvements in the management of global supply chains. For international business, AI helps to reduce the liability of foreignness by improving communication and also by deepening the understanding of the consumption patterns of overseas consumers.

Having said this, the three global frameworks (US, EU, and China) for the handling of data are reducing the possibilities of growth based on improvements from technological developments. This is mainly because politics and geopolitics are taking prevalence over business, economics, and technology development. Countries are increasingly focused on their digital sovereignty to complement their analogue sovereignty. As new technologies will be generating new sources of growth, transformation in industries, and increases in productivity, countries intend to reap the benefits of setting the standards and therefore dominating global markets. This is known as "splinternet". These three different data handling frameworks are adding to the increasing politically fueled fragmentation of the world market into two blocks.

7.2   What's Next?

The analysis and discussion in this book started in a period where globalization was growing as a result of lowering trade barriers and major technological developments. This growth in international trade was mainly led by companies based in advanced economies after more than a century of industrial agglomeration, growth, and wealth accumulation that came after both steam power and international peace reduced the barriers to international trade. At the end of the 1900s, these companies enjoyed an advantage in terms of technology, knowledge, access to money, and access to markets. In fact, between 1820 and 1990 the share of income heading to advanced economies grew from 20% to almost 70%. This is known as the Great Divergence (Baldwin, 2016).

But since the 1990s, the percentage going to advanced economies has returned to 1900s levels. This is the result of industrialization and transportation improvements that led to "trade in goods". Then technological developments made profitable to move manufacturing operations to low labor cost locations, which led to "trade in factories". More recently, widespread internet access has allowed work to take place at home, in the US, in India, or in Bali, which led to "trade in offices" (Wolf, 2022). This has meant a rapid industrialization of a few emerging economies and the simultaneous deindustrialization of advanced economies; these along with a commodity supercycle during the last 10+ years has resulted in today's Great Convergence (Baldwin, 2016).

Within this context, one of the future challenges is the widening gap in the adoption and implementation of technological developments among countries, companies, and workers; a gap that is forecasted to bring unbalanced benefits. As the world is moving towards two trade blocks, knowledge flows will be limited and therefore global growth hindered (and probably growth will be more concentrated in technology leading countries). Another challenge is what Baldwin (2020) called the "globotics upheaval"; the combination of globalization and robotics supported by computing power that is challenging humans' monopoly on thinking. Therefore AI models will be increasingly competing for white-collar jobs, which could pose a threat to the foundations of liberal welfare states.

Technology developments have brought the world closer mainly as a result of technological improvements since the Industrial Revolution. After all, "healthy global trade is a sign of peace" (Wolf, 2022). However, now the disputes over the dominance of these technologies and of the digital sovereignty are fragmenting the world (along with disruptive events such as wars or the current energy crisis). This presents a context with high uncertainties. In the past, economic forces have been the main driver shaping globalization, and as such it can be expected that they will continue to play a major role, although they will be operating in an environment with strong political forces that likely will result in a diversification of supply chains and production centers.

New technologies will become mainstream, following the path of AI, and will create a major impact in the economy and also in the possibilities for international expansion. These technologies will create major business opportunities in areas like energy, transportation, energy storage/batteries, edge computing, human-computer interfaces, 3D printing, or genomics. At the same time, new regulations will be in place, and they will also [re]shape the industries. We can only hope that they bring a more level playing field rather than maintaining the fragmentation and bias we are currently seeing.

Finally, globalization and technology have proved to reduce the wealth gap in the world. Despite the challenges mentioned above, there are still many opportunities to keep increasing living standards across the world through technological developments and economic integration. The most impactful will probably be giving access to health and education to places where they have not been easily available. This should be the main task for governments, companies, and societies for the next 10+ years.

References

Baldwin, R. (2016). *The great convergence. Information technology and the new globalization.* Massachusetts, Harvard University Press.

Baldwin, R. (2020). *The Globotics upheaval. Globalization, robotics, and the future of work.* Oxford University Press.

WTO. (2022). Statistics on trade in commercial services. Retrieved from https://www.wto.org/english/res_e/statis_e/tradeserv_stat_e.htm

References

Aagaard, A. (Ed.). (2019). *Digital business models. Driving transformation and innovation.* Palgrave Macmillan.

Accenture Research. (2021). *The art of AI maturity. Advancing from practice to performance.* Retrieved from https://www.accenture.com/us-en/insights/artificial-intelligence/ai-maturity-and-transformation.

Adamson, A., & Smith, A. (2018). Machine learning and health care disparities in dermatology. *JAMA Dermatology, 154*(11), 1. https://doi.org/10.1001/jamadermatol.2018.2348

Ahmed, U. (2019). The importance of Cross-border regulatory cooperation in an era of digital trade. *World Trade Review, 18*(S1), S99–S120. https://doi.org/10.1017/S1474745618000514

Alan, A. A., Noemi, S., Yelnur, S., Rudolf, R. S., & Nikolay, M. (2022). Advanced technologies and international business: A multidisciplinary analysis of the literature. *International Business Review, 31*(4), 101967. https://doi.org/10.1016/j.ibusrev.2021.101967

Altamira, M. (2021). *The role of home institutions in the development of marketing capabilities. Competitive advantages at home and abroad in Chinese companies expanding their operations in the European Union.* (PhD). University of Warwick, United Kingdom.

© The Author(s), under exclusive license to Springer Nature Switzerland AG 2023   **113**
G. Fornes, M. Altamira, *Digitalization, Technology and Global Business,*
https://doi.org/10.1007/978-3-031-33111-4

Altamira, M., Fornes, G., & Mendez, A. (2022). Chinese institutions and international expansion within the Belt and Road Initiative: firm capabilities of Chinese companies in the European Union. *Asia Pacific Business Review.* doi: https://doi.org/10.1080/13602381.2022.2093520

Altman, S., & Bastian, C. (2021). The state of globalization in 2021. *Harvard Business Review.* Retrieved from https://hbr.org/2021/03/the-state-of-globalization-in-2021

Alvarez-Risco, A., & Del-Aguila-Arcentales, S. (2021). A note on changing regulation in international business: The world intellectual property organization (WIPO) and artificial intelligence. In A. Verbeke, R. van Tulder, E. L. Rose, & Y. Wei (Eds.), *The multiple dimensions of institutional complexity in international business research* (Vol. 15, pp. 363–371). Emerald Publishing Limited.

Andrea, S., & Andrea De, M. (2021). Leveraging artificial intelligence in business: Implications, applications and methods. *Technology Analysis & Strategic Management,* *34*(1), 16–29. https://doi.org/10.1080/09537325.2021.1883583

Arvidsson, H. G. S., & Arvidsson, R. (2019). The Uppsala model of internationalisation and beyond. *International Journal of Finance and Administration,* *42*(2), 221–239.

Asian Development Bank. (2022). *Promoting Digitalization for Green and Inclusive Growth in Asia.* Retrieved from Regional (INO, KOR, MAL, PHI, PRC, SIN, THA, VIE).

Aslam, A., Eugster, J., Ho, G., Jaumotte, F., Osorio-Buitron, C., & Piazza, R. (2018). Globalization helps spread knowledge and technology across borders. Retrieved from https://www.imf.org/en/Blogs/Articles/2018/04/09/globalization-helps-spread-knowledge-and-technology-across-borders.

Avendaño, T. (2019, 2 August 2019). 'La casa de papel' logra más de 34 millones de espectadores y refuerza la estrategia internacional de Netflix. *El Pais.* Retrieved from https://elpais.com/cultura/2019/08/01/television/1564671328_371797.html

Balakrishnan, T., Chui, M., & Henke, N. (2020). *The state of AI in 2020.* Retrieved from https://www.mckinsey.com/capabilities/quantumblack/our-insights/global-survey-the-state-of-ai-in-2020

Baldwin, R. (2016). *The great convergence. Information technology and the new globalization.* Massachusets Harvard University Press.

Baldwin, R. (2020). *The Globotics upheaval. Globalization, robotics, and the future of work.* Oxford University Press.

Banalieva, E. R., & Dhanaraj, C. (2019). Internationalization theory for the digital economy. *Journal of International Business Studies, 50,* 1372–1387.

Barney, J. (1991). Firm resources and sustained competitive advantage. *Journal of Management, 17*(1), 99–120.

Barney, J., Wright, M., & Ketchen, D. (2001). The resource-based view of the firm: Ten years after 1991. *Journal of Management, 27*, 625–641.

Barrutia, J. M., & Echebarria, C. (2007). A new internet driven internationalisation framework. *The Service Industries Journal, 27*(7), 923–946.

Beattie, A. (2018). Data protectionism: the growing menace to global business. *Financial Times.* Retrieved from https://www.ft.com/content/6f0f41e4-47de-11e8-8ee8-cae73aab7ccb.

Boisot, M., & Meyer, M. (2008). Which way through the open door? Reflections on the internationalization of Chinese firms. *Management and Organization Review, 4*(3), 349–365.

Brache, J., & Felzensztein, C. (2019). Exporting firm's engagement with trade associations: Insights from Chile. *International Business Review, 28*, 25–35.

Brakman, S., Garretsen, H., van Marrewijk, C., & van Witteloostuijn, A. (2006). *Nations and firms in the global economy. An introduction to international economics and business.* Cambridge University Press.

Brouthers, K., Geisser, K., & Rothlauf, F. (2016). Explaining the internationalization of ibusiness firms. *Journal of International Business Studies, 47*(5), 513–534.

Brynjolfsson, E., Hui, X., & Liu, M. (2019). Does machine translation affect international trade? Evidence from a large digital platform. *Management Science, 65*(12), 5449–5460. https://doi.org/10.1287/mnsc.2019.3388

Buckley, P. (2018). Internalisation theory and outward direct investment by emerging market multinationals. *Management International Review, 58*, 195–224.

Buckley, P. J. (2020). The theory and empirics of the structural reshaping of globalization. *Journal of International Business Studies, 51*(9), 1580–1592. https://doi.org/10.1057/s41267-020-00355-5

Buckley, P., & Casson, M. (1976). *The future of the multinational enterprise.* Macmillan.

Buckley, P., Clegg, J., Cross, A., Liu, X., Voss, H., & Zheng, P. (2007). The determinants of Chinese outward foreign direct investment. *Journal of International Business Studies, 38*(4), 499–518.

Buckley, P., Clegg, J., Voss, H., Cross, A., Liu, X., & Zheng, P. (2018). A retrospective and agenda for future research on Chinese outward foreign direct investment. *Journal of International Business Studies, 49*, 4–23.

Bughin, J., Seong, J., Manyika, J., Chui, M., & Joshi, R. (2018). *Notes from the AI frontier modeling the impact of AI on the world economy.* Mckinsey Global

Institute. Retrieved from https://www.mckinsey.com/~/media/McKinsey/ Featured%20Insights/Artificial%20Intelligence/Notes%20from%20 the%20frontier%20Modeling%20the%20impact%20of%20AI%20on%20 the%20world%20economy/MGI-Notes-from-the-AI-frontier-Modeling-the-impact-of-AI-on-the-world-economy-September-2018.ashx

Bughin, J., Catlin, T., & Dietz, M. (2019). The right digital-platform strategy. *McKinsey Quarterly, 2*, 1–4.

Cai, Z., Poulos, R., Liu, J., & Zhong, Q. (2022). Machine learning for multi-omics data integration in cancer. *iScience, 25*(2), 1. https://doi.org/10.1016/j. isci.2022.103798

Calhoun, M. (2002). Unpacking liability of foreignness: Identifying culturally driven external and internal sources of liability for the foreign subsidiary. *Journal of International Management, 8*(3), 301–321.

Camison, C., & Villar-Lopez, A. (2010). Effect of SMEs international experience on foreign intensity and economic performance: The mediating role of internationally exploitable assets and competitive strategy. *Journal of Small Business Management, 48*, 116–151.

Cardoza, G., & Fornes, G. (2011). The internationalisation of SMEs from China: The case of Ningxia Hui autonomous region. *Asia Pacific Journal of Management, 28*(4), 737–759.

Cardoza, G., Fornes, G., Li, P., Xu, N., & Xu, S. (2015). China goes global: Public policies' influence on small- and medium-sized enterprises' international expansion. *Asia Pacific Business Review, 21*(2), 188–210.

Cardoza, G., Fornes, G., Farber, V., Gonzalez Duarte, R., & Ruiz Gutierrez, J. (2016). Barriers and public policies affecting the international expansion of Latin American SMEs. Evidence from Brazil, Colombia, and Peru. *Journal of Business Research, 69*(6), 2030–2039.

Casalini, F., & Lopez Gonzalez, J. (2019). Trade and Cross-Border Data Flows. *OECD Trade Policy Papers* (220). doi: 10.1787/18166873.

Casson, M. (2000). *Economics of international business*. Edward Elgar.

Caves, R. (1971). International corporations: The industrial economics of foreign investment. *Economica, 38*, 1.

Caves, R. (1974). Industrial Organization. In J. Dunning (Ed.), *Economic analysis and the multinational Enterprise*. Allen & Unwin.

Cavusgil, S., & Zou, S. (1994). Marketing strategy - performance relationship: An investigation of the empirical link in export market ventures. *Journal of Marketing, 58*, 1–21.

Chappell, J. (2020). *Artificial Intelligence: From predictive to prescriptive and beyond*. Retrieved from https://insource.solutions/wp-content/

uploads/2020/05/WhitePaper_AIfromPredictivetoPrescriptiveandB eyond-EN.pdf

Chen, H., & Chen, T. (1998). Network linkages and location choice in foreign direct investment. *Journal of International Business Studies, 29*(3), 1.

Child, J., & Marinova, S. (2014). The role of contextual combinations in the globalization of Chinese firms. *Management and Organization Review, 10*(3), 347–371.

Child, J., & Rodrigues, S. (2005). The internationalization of Chinese firms: A case for theoretical extension? *Management and Organization Review, 1*(3), 381–410.

Chin, Y.-C., & Zhao, J. (2022). Governing Cross-border data flows: International trade agreements and their limits. *Laws, 11*(4), 63. Retrieved from https:// www.mdpi.com/2075-471X/11/4/63

Colao, V. (2015). Speech at the World Economic Forum.

Colback, L. (2020a, 28 February 2020). How to navigate the US-China trade war. Global supply chains are at risk as the world's two biggest economies threaten to decouple. *Financial Times.* Retrieved from https://www.ft.com/ content/6124beb8-5724-11ea-abe5-8e03987b7b20

Colback, L. (2020b). The impact of AI on business and society. *Financial Times.* Retrieved from https://www.ft.com/content/e082b01d-fbd6-4ea5-a0d2-05bc5ad7176c.

Collinson, S. C., & Narula, R. (2014). Asset recombination in international partnerships as a source of improved innovation capabilities in China. *The Multinational Business Review, 22*(4), 394–417. https://doi.org/10.1108/ MBR-09-2014-0046

Computer History Museum. (2022). Fellowship for Prof Tim Berners-Lee for his seminal contributions to the development of the World Wide Web. Retrieved from https://computerhistory.org/profile/tim-berners-lee/

Conner, K., & Prahalad, C. (1996). A resource-based theory of the firm: Knowledge versus opportunism. *Organization Science, 7*(5), 477–501.

Costa, E., Soares, A. L., & De Sousa, J. P. (2016). Information, knowledge and collaboration management in the internationalisation of SMEs: A systematic literature review. *International Journal of Information Management, 36*(4), 557–569.

Costa, E., Soares, A., & Pinho de Sousa, J. (2019). On the use of digital platforms to support SME internationalization in the context of industrial business associations. doi: https://doi.org/10.4018/978-1-5225-6225-2.ch004.

Coviello, N., Liena, K., & Liesch, P. (2017). Adapting the Uppsala model to a modern world: Macro-context and microfoundations. *Journal of International Business Studies, 48*, 1151–1164.

Cuervo-Cazurra, Á., Maloney, M., & Manrakhan, S. (2007). Causes of the difficulties in internationalization. *Journal of International Business Studies, 38*, 709–725.

Davis, L., & North, D. (1971). *Institutional change and American economic growth*. Cambridge University Press.

Daza Jaller, L., Gaillard, S., & Molinuevo, M. (2020). The regulation of Digital Trade. Key policies and international trends. In. Washington: World Bank.

Delios, A., & Beamish, P. (2001). Survival and profitability: The roles of experience and intangible assets in foreign subsidiary performance. *Academy of Management Journal, 44*, 1028–1038.

Deloitte. (2022). *Using autonomous robots to drive supply chain innovation.* Retrieved from https://www2.deloitte.com/us/en/pages/manufacturing/articles/autonomous-robots-supply-chain-innovation.html

Deng, P. (2011). The internationalization of Chinese firms: a critical review and future research. *International Journal of Management Reviews, DOI:* https://doi.org/10.1111/j.1468-2370.2011.00323.x.

Díaz-Guerra, I. (2019, 12 September 2019). Javier Gómez Santander: "Los españoles no somos un buen ejército, pero como guerrilla somos la hostia". *El Mundo*. Retrieved from https://www.elmundo.es/papel/cultura/2019/09/12/5d791951fc6c8337538b45fe.html

Díaz-Infante, N., Lazar, M., Ram, S., & Ray, A. (2022, 20 July 2022). Demand for online education is growing. Are providers ready? *McKinsey & Company.* Retrieved from https://www.mckinsey.com/industries/education/our-insights/demand-for-online-education-is-growing-are-providers-ready

Doz, Y., Asakawa, K., Santos, J., & Williamson, P. (1997). The metanational corporation. *INSEAD working paper.*

Dunning, J. (1977). Trade, location of economic activity, and the MNE: A search for an eclectic approach. In B. Ohlin, P. O. Hesselborn, & P. M. Wijkman (Eds.), *The international allocation of economic activity*. Macmillan.

Dunning, J. (1995). Reappraising the eclectic paradigm in the age of alliance capitalism. *Journal of International Business Studies, 26*, 1.

Dunning, J. (1996). The geographical sources of competitiveness of firms: The results of a new survey. *Transnational Corporations, 5*(3), 1.

Dunning, J. (2001a). The eclectic (OLI) paradigm of international production: Past, present, and future. *Journal of the Economics of Business, 8*(2), 1.

Dunning, J. H. (2001b). *Oxford handbook of international business*. Oxford University Press.

Dunning, J. (2003). Some antecedents of internalization theory. *Journal of International Business Studies, 34*(2), 108–115.

Dunning, J. H. (2015). *The eclectic paradigm of international production: A restatement and some possible extensions*. Palgrave Macmillan.

Dunning, J., & Lundan, S. (1998). The geographical sources of competitiveness. *International Business Review, 7*(2), 1.

Enright, M. (1998). Regional clusters and firm strategy. In A. Chandler, P. Hagstrom, & O. Solvell (Eds.), *The dynamic firm*. Oxford University Press.

Enright, M. (2000). The globalization of competition and the localization of competitive advantages: Policies towards regional clustering. In N. Hood & S. Young (Eds.), *The globalization of multinational Enterprise activity*. Macmillan.

Espinoza, J. (2022a). EU to unveil landmark legislation to tackle market power of Big Tech. *Financial Times*. Retrieved from https://www.ft.com/content/1c66027d-717f-4d71-b76b-34077721a678.

Espinoza, J. (2022b). EU to unveil law to force Big Tech to police illegal content. *Financial Times*. Retrieved from https://www.ft.com/content/f39a8b61-c7b4-4674-9606-b923f63ad770.

Estrin, S., & Prevezer, M. (2011). The role of informal institutions in corporate governance: Brazil, Russia, India, and China compared. *Asia Pacific Journal of Management, 28*(1), 41–67.

European Commission. (2022a). Digital Skills and Jobs. Retrieved from https://digital-strategy.ec.europa.eu/en/policies/digital-skills-and-jobs

European Commission. (2022b). *The digital markets act: Ensuring fair and open digital markets*. European Commission.

European Parliament. (2020). *Legal analysis of international trade law and digital trade*. Policy Department for External Relations.

eWTP. (2022). Who we are. Retrieved from https://www.ewtp.org/

Ferencz, J., López-González, J., & Oliván, I. (2022). Artifical intelligence and international trade. Some preliminary implications. *OECD Trade Policy, 260*. Retrieved from https://www.oecd-ilibrary.org/docserver/13212d3e-en.pdf?e xpires=1667908068&id=id&accname=guest&checksum=9015F2532974C 3E24F619FA3A636AA81

Financial Times Reporters. (2022). How the US chip export controls have turned the screws on China. *Financial Times*. Retrieved from https://www.ft.com/content/bbbdc7dc-0566-4a05-a7b3-27afd82580f3.

Fink, M. (2020). Legal analysis of international trade law and digital trade. *Think Tank European Parliament.* doi:10.2861/137398.

Florida, R. (1995). Towards the learning region. *Futures, 27,* 1.

Floridi, L. (2020). The fight for digital Sovereignity: What it is, and why it matters, especially for the EU. *Philosophy & Technology, 33,* 369–378. https://link.springer.com/article/10.1007/s13347-020-00423-6.

Fornes, G. (2009). *Foreign exchange exposure in emerging markets. How companies can minimize it.* Palgrave Macmillan.

Fornes, G., & Butt Philip, A. (2014). Chinese outward investments to emerging markets. Evidence from Latin America. *European Business Review, 26*(6), 1.

Fornes, G., & Cardoza, G. (2018). Internationalization of Chinese SMEs: The perception of disadvantages of foreignness. *Emerging Markets Finance and Trade.* https://doi.org/10.1080/1540496X.2018.1518218

Fornes, G., & Cardoza, G. (2019). Internationalization of Chinese SMEs: The perception of disadvantages of foreignness. *Emerging Markets Finance and Trade, 55*(9), 2086–2105.

Fornes, G., & Mendez, A. (2018). *The China-Latin America Axis. Emerging markets and their role in an increasingly globalised world.* Palgrave Macmillan.

Fornes, G., & Rovira, J. (2020). Emerging economies and the Covid-19 crisis. In G. L. Gardini (Ed.), *The world before and after Covid-19.* European Institute of International Studies Press.

Fornes, G., Monfort, A., Ilie, C., Koo, C. K., & Cardoza, G. (2019). Ethics, responsibility, and sustainability in MBAs. Understanding the motivations for the incorporation of ERS in less traditional markets. *Sustainability, 11,* 1.

Fornes, G., Cardoza, G., & Altamira, M. (2021). Do political and business relations help emerging markets' SMEs in their national and international expansion? Evidence from Brazil and China. *International Journal of Emerging Markets.* doi: https://doi.org/10.1108/IJOEM-01-2020-0058

Fortune. (2022). The electronic World Trade Platform: making global trade more inclusive. *Fortune.* Retrieved from https://brand-studio.fortune.com/alibaba-group/making-global-trade-more-inclusive/?prx_t=dT8HAzi5SAoPEQA&spm=a2o7pe.23809426

G20 2016. (2016). G20 Leaders' Communique Hangzhou Summit. Retrieved from http://www.g20chn.org/English/Dynamic/201609/t20160906_3396.html

Garcia-Macia, D., & Goyal, R. (2021). Decoupling in the digital era. *Finance & Development. International Monetary Fund.* Retrieved from https://www.imf.

org/external/pubs/ft/fandd/2021/03/international-cooperation-and-the-digital-economy-garcia.htm.

GHD. (2022). Ten emerging trends shaping our new future. Retrieved from https://www.ghd.com/en/perspectives/ten-emerging-trends-shaping-our-new-future.aspx

Goel, S., & Karri, R. (2006). Entrepreneurs, Effectual Logic, and Over-Trust *Entrepreneurship Theory and Practice.*

Gonzalez, C. (2022). Bizarrap and Quevedo Achieve the #1 Song on Spotify's Global Top. Retrieved from https://www.jefebet.com/en/featured/bizarrap-and-quevedo-achieve-the-1-song-on-spotifys-global-top/

Harford, T. (2014, 28 March 2014). Big data: Are we making a big mistake? *Financial Times.*

He, S., Khan, Z., Lew, Y., & Fallon, G. (2019). Technological innovation as a source of Chinese multinationals' firm-specific advantages and international-ization. *International Journal of Emerging Markets, 14*(4), 1. https://doi.org/10.1108/IJOEM-02-2017-0059

Hennart, J.-F. (2019). Digitalized service multinationals andinternational business theory. *Journal of International Business Studies, 50*(8), 1388–1400. https://doi.org/10.1057/s41267-019-00256-2

Hervé, A., Schmitt, C., & Baldegger, R. (2020). Internationalization and digitalization: Applying digital technologies to the internationalization process of small and medium-sized enterprises. *Technology Innovation Management Review, 10*(7), 28–40.

Hofstede, G. (1981). Culture and organizations. *International Studies of Management and Organization, 10*(4), 15–41.

Hoskisson, R. E., Eden, L., Lau, C. M., & Wright, M. (2000). Strategy in emerging economies. *Academy of Management Journal, 43*(3), 249–267.

Huijun, J., & Fiona, H. (2022). Exploring the impact of digital platforms on SME internationalization: New Zealand SMEs use of the Alibaba platform for Chinese market entry. *Journal of Asia-Pacific Business, 19*(2), 72–95. https://doi.org/10.1080/10599231.2018.1453743

Hymer, S. (1960). *The international operations of national firms: A study of foreign direct investment.* MIT Press.

Hymer, S. (1968). La grande 'corporation' multinationale: Analyse de certaines raisons qui poussant à l'intégration internationale des affaires. *Reveu Economique, 14*(6), 1.

IMF. (2019). *World economic outlook.* Retrieved from https://www.imf.org/en/Publications/WEO/Issues/2019/03/28/world-economic-outlook-april-2019#Chapter%202

IMF. (2020). *Global outlook update.* World Bank.

Jean, R.-J. B., & Kim, D. (2020). Internet and SMEs' internationalization: The role of platform and website. *Journal of International Management, 26*(1), 100690. https://doi.org/10.1016/j.intman.2019.100690

Jean, R.-J. B., Kim, D., & Cavusgil, E. (2020). Antecedents and outcomes of digital platform risk for international new ventures' internationalization. *Journal of World Business, 55*(1), 101021. https://doi.org/10.1016/j.jwb.2019.101021

Jin, H., & Hurd, F. (2018). Exploring the impact of digital platforms on SME internationalization: New Zealand SMEs use of the Alibaba platform for Chinese market entry. *Journal of Asia-Pacific Business, 19*(2), 72–95. https://doi.org/10.1080/10599231.2018.1453743

Johanson, J., & Vahlne, J. (1977). The internationalization process of the firm. A model of knowledge development and increasing foreign market commitments. *Journal of International Business Studies, 8,* 23–32.

Johanson, J., & Vahlne, J. (2009). The Upssala internationalization process model revisited: From liability of foreignness to liability of outsidership. *Journal of International Business Studies, 40*(9), 1411–1431.

Kapoor, V. (2021, 23 July 2021). How Netflix uses big data for consumer satisfaction. *The Economic Tribune.* Retrieved from https://www.econtribune.com/post/how-netflix-uses-big-data-for-customer-satisfaction

Karhunen, P., Kosonen, R., McCarthy, D., & Puffer, S. (2018). The darker side of social networks in transforming economies: Corrupt exchange in Chinese guanxi and Russian Blat/Svyazi. *Management and Organization Review, 14*(2), 395–419.

Kavadias, S., Ladas, K., & Loch, C. (2016). The transformative business model. How to tell if you have one. *Harvard Business Review, October.*

Khan, S. A. R., Piprani, A. Z., & Yu, Z. (2022). Supply chain analytics and post-pandemic performance: mediating role of triple-A supply chain strategies. *International Journal of Emerging Markets, ahead-of-print*(ahead-of-print). doi:https://doi.org/10.1108/IJOEM-11-2021-1744.

Khanna, T., & Palepu, K. (1997). Why focused strategies may be wrong for emerging markets. *Harvard Business Review, 4*(75), 3–10.

Khanna, T., & Palepu, K. (2000). The future of business groups in emerging markets: Long-run evidence from Chile. *Academy of Management Journal, 43*(3), 268–285.

Khanna, T., & Palepu, K. (2010). *Winning in emerging markets: A road map for strategy and execution.* Harvard Business School Publishing Corporation.

Kittilaksanawong, W. (2017). Institutional distances, resources and entry strategies: Evidence from newly industrialized economy firms. *International Journal of Emerging Markets, 12*(1), 58–78. https://doi.org/10.1108/IJoEM-12-2014-0196

Kobrin, S. J. (2017). Bricks and mortar in a borderless world: Globalization, the backlash, and the multinational Enterprise. *Global Strategy Journal, 7*(2), 159–171. https://doi.org/10.1002/gsj.1158

Kogut, B., & Kulatilaka, N. (1994). Operational flexibility, global manufacturing, and the option value of a multinational network. *Management Science, 40,* 1.

Kogut, B., & Singh, H. (1988). The effect of national culture on the choice of entry mode. *Journal of International Business Studies, 19*(3), 411–432.

Kogut, B., & Zander, I. (1994). Knowledge of the firm and the evolutionary theory of the multinational corporation. *Journal of International Business Studies, 24*(4), 1.

Kojima, K. (1982). Macro economic versus international business approaches to foreign direct investments. *Hotosubashi Journal of Economics, 23,* 1.

Kuemmerle, W. (1999). The drivers of foreign direct investment into research and development: An empirical investment. *Journal of International Business Studies, 30*(1), 1.

Larrazabal, A., Nieto, N., Peterson, V., Milone, D., & Ferrante, E. (2020). Gender imbalance in medical imaging datasets produces biased classifiers for computer-aided diagnosis. *PNAS, 117*(23), 1. https://www.pnas.org/doi/full/10.1073/pnas.1919012117.

Lee, D. (2021, 29 July 2021). A Tesla for every referral' as start-ups buy Amazon's top sellers. *Financial Times.*

Leonidou, L. (2004). An analysis of the barriers hindering small business export development. *Journal of Small Business Management, 42*(3), 279–302.

Li, J., Pan, Y., Yang, Y., & Tse, C. H. (2022). Digital platform attention and international sales: An attention-based view. *Journal of International Business Studies.* https://doi.org/10.1057/s41267-022-00528-4

Li-Hua, R. (2007). What is technology management? *Journal of Technology Management in China, 2*(1), 1. https://doi.org/10.1108/jtmc.2007.30202aaa.001

Lippoldt, D. (2022). *Regulating the Digital Economy: Reflections on the Trade and Innovation Nexus.* Paper presented at the Project for Peaceful Competition:

Global Cooperation on Digital Governance and the Geoeconomics of New Technologies in a Multi-polar World, Virtual. https://www.cigionline.org/articles/regulating-the-digital-economy-reflections-on-the-trade-and-innovation-nexus/

Loane, S. (2005). The role of the internet in the internationalisation of small and medium sized companies. *Journal of International Entrepreneurship, 3*(4), 263–277.

Loureiro, S., Guerreiro, J., & Iis, T. (2021). Artificial intelligence in business: State of the art and future research agenda. *Journal of Business Research, 129*, 911–926. https://doi.org/10.1016/j.jbusres.2020.11.001

Lucas, L. (2017, 22 March 2017). Alibaba kicks off ambitious plan for frontier-free global trade. *Financial Times.*

Luo, Y. (2021). New OLI advantages in digital globalization. *International Business Review, 30*, 1. https://doi.org/10.1016/j.ibusrev.2021.101797

Luo, X., Wang, Y., & Zhang, X. (2019). E-Commerce development and household consumption growth in China. *World Bank Policy Research Working Paper*(8810).

Ma, J. (2018). Speech at the World Economic Forum.

Malmberg, A., Solvell, O., & Zander, I. (1996). Spatial clustering, local accumulation of knowledge and firm competitiveness. *Geographical Annals, 78*(2), 1.

Manisha, N. (2022). Asian Development Bank, Asian economic integration report 2022: Advancing digital services trade in Asia and the Pacific, Asian Development Bank, 2022, 300 pp., \$51 (paperback). ISBN: 978-92-9269-361-9 (print), ISBN: 978-92-9269-362-6 (electronic), 978-92-9269-363-3 (eBook). *Journal of Asian Economic Integration, 4*(2), 211–213. https://doi.org/10.1177/26316846221107416

Marr, B. (2022). What is the impact of Artificial Intelligence (AI) On Society? Retrieved from https://bernardmarr.com/what-is-the-impact-of-artificial-intelligence-ai-on-society/#:~:text=Artificial%20intelligence%20can%20dramatically%20improve,creativity%20and%20empathy%20among%20others.

Mathews, J. (2006). Dragon multinationals: New players in 21st century globalization. *Asia Pacific Journal of Management, 23*(1), 5–27.

Mathews, J. (2017). Dragon multinationals powered by linkage, leverage and learning: A review and development. *Asia Pacific Journal of Management, 34*, 769–777.

Mathews, J. (2018). Dragon multinationals powered by linkage, leverage and learning: A review and development. *Asia Pacific Journal of Management, 34,* 769–775.

McDonald, F., & Burton, F. (2002). *International business.* Thomson.

McManus, J. (1972). The theory of the international firm. In G. Paquet (Ed.), *The multinational firm and the nation state.* Collins and Macmillan.

Meltzer, J. (2018, 13 December 2018). The impact of artificial intelligence on international trade. *Brookings.* Retrieved from https://www.brookings.edu/research/the-impact-of-artificial-intelligence-on-international-trade/.

Meltzer, J. P. (2019). Governing digital trade. *World Trade Review, 18*(S1), S23–S48. https://doi.org/10.1017/S1474745618000502

Melzer, J. (2018). *The impact of artificial intelligence on international trade.* Retrieved from https://www.brookings.edu/research/the-impact-of-artificial-intelligence-on-international-trade/

Meyer, K., & Peng, M. (2016). Theoretical foundations of emerging economy business research. *Journal of International Business Studies, 47,* 3–22. https://doi.org/10.1057/jibs.2015.34

Moon, H. (1999). *An unconventional theory of foreign direct investment.* Seoul National University.

Narula, R., Asmussen, C. G., Chi, T., & Kundu, S. K. (2019). Applying and advancing internalization theory: The multinational enterprise in the twenty-first century. *Journal of International Business Studies, 50*(8), 1231–1252. https://doi.org/10.1057/s41267-019-00260-6

Netflix. (2022). Most Popular TV (Non-English). Retrieved from https://top10.netflix.com/tv-non-english

Neufeld, D. (2021). Long Waves: The History of Innovation Cycles. Retrieved from https://www.visualcapitalist.com/the-history-of-innovation-cycles/

North, D. (1984). Transaction costs, institutions, and economic history. *Journal of Institutional and Theoretical Economics, 140,* 7–17.

North, D. (1990). *Institutions, institutional change, and economic performance.* Cambridge University Press.

North, D. (1991). Institutions. *The Journal of Economic Perspectives, 5*(1), 97–112.

North, D. (1993). The new institutional economics and development. Retrieved from Http://econwpa.wustl.edu:8089/eps/eh/papers/9309/9309001.pdf

North, D. (1995). Five propositions about institutional change. In J. Knight & I. Sened (Eds.), *Exploring social institutions.* University of Michigan Press.

North, D. (2005). *Understanding the process of economic change.* Princeton University Press.

OECD. (2013). *OECD guidelines on the protection of privacy and transborder flows of personal data.* Retrieved from Paris https://www.oecd.org/sti/ieconomy/oecdguidelinesontheprotectionofprivacyandtransborderflowsofpersonaldata.htm

OECD. (2022a). *OECD studies on SMEs and entrepreneurship.* OECDilibrary.

OECD. (2022b). SMEs and enterpreneurship. Retrieved from https://www.oecd.org/cfe/smes/

Ojala, A., Evers, N., & Sousa, C. (2022). Digitalisation, digital services and companies' internationalisation. In *Sustainable international business models in a digitally transformed world.* Routledge.

Oliveira, R., Figueira, A., & Pinhanez, M. (2018). Uppsala model: A contingent theory to explain the rise of EMNEs. *Revista Eletrônica de Negócios Internacionais, 13*(2), 30–42.

Park, S., & Luo, Y. (2001). Guanxi and organizational dynamics: Organizational networking in Chinese firms. *Strategic Management Journal, 22*(5), 455–477.

Peng, M., Lee, S.-H., & Wang, D. (2005). What determines the scope of the firm over time? A focus on institutional relatedness. *Academy of Management Review, 30*(3), 622–633.

Peng, M., Wang, D., & Jiang, Y. (2008). An institution-based view of international business strategy: A focus on emerging economies. *Journal of International Business Studies, 39*, 920–936.

Peng, M., Lebedev, S., Vlas, C., Wang, J., & Shay, J. (2018). The growth of the firm in (and out of) emerging economies. *Asia Pacific Journal of Management, 35*(4), 829–857.

Penrose, E. (1959). *The theory of the growth of the firm.* Sharpe.

Petersen, B., Welch, L. S., & Liesch, P. W. (2002). *The internet and foreign market expansion by firms* (pp. 207–221). MIR: Management International Review.

Petricevic, O., & Teece, D. J. (2019). The structural reshaping of globalization: Implications for strategic sectors, profiting from innovation, and the multinational enterprise. *Journal of International Business Studies, 50*(9), 1487–1512. https://doi.org/10.1057/s41267-019-00269-x

Pollman, E., & Barry, J. (2017). Regulatory entrepreneurship. *Southern California Law Review, 90*, 383–448.

Porter, M. (1998). Clusters and competition: New agendas for companies, governments, and institutions. In M. Porter (Ed.), *On competition.* Harvard Business School Press.

PWC. (2017). Sizing the prize. PWC's Global Artificial Intelligence Study: Exploiting the AI Revolution. Retrieved from https://www.pwc.com/gx/en/issues/analytics/assets/pwc-ai-analysis-sizing-the-prize-report.pdf

Qu, Y. J., Ming, X. G., Liu, Z. W., Zhang, X. Y., & Hou, Z. T. (2019). Smart manufacturing systems: State of the art and future trends. *The International Journal of Advanced Manufacturing Technology, 103*(9), 3751–3768. https://doi.org/10.1007/s00170-019-03754-7

Ramamurti, R. (2012). What is really different about emerging market multinationals? *Global Strategy Journal, 2*(1), 41–47.

Rauch, J., & Trindade, V. (2002). Ethnic Chinese networks in international trade. *The Review of Economics and Statistics, February, 1,* 116–130.

Rhee, J. H. (2005). The internet era and the international expansion process: The moderating role of absorptive capacity. *MIR: Management International Review, 1,* 277–306.

Rottig, D. (2016). Institutions and emerging markets: Effects and implications for multinational corporations. *International Journal of Emerging Markets, 11*(1), 2–17.

Ruan, J. (2017). *Guanxi, social capital and school choice in China. The rise of ritual capital.* Palgrave Macmillan.

Rugman, A., & Li, J. (2007). Will China's multinationals succeed globally or regionally? *European Management Journal, 25*(5), 333–343.

Ruiz-Real, J. L., Uribe-Toril, J., Torres, J. A., & De Pablo, J. (2021). Artificial intelligence in business and economics research: Trends and future. *Journal of Business Economics and Management, 22*(1), 98–117. https://doi.org/10.3846/jbem.2020.13641

Schmidt, E. (2015). Speech at the World Economic Forum.

Schonberger, V., & Ramge, T. (2018). *Reinventing capitalism in the age of big data.* Basic Books.

Scoglio, A. A., Reilly, E. D., Gorman, J. A., & Drebing, C. E. (2019). Use of social robots in mental health and well-being research: Systematic review. *Journal of Medical Internet Research, 21*(7), e13322. https://doi.org/10.2196/13322

Sebastian, I., Ross, J., Beath, C., Mocker, M., Moloney, K., & Fonstad, N. (2020). How big old companies navigate digital transformation. In R. Galliers, D. Leidner, & B. Simeonova (Eds.), *Strategic information management. Theory and practice* (5th ed.). Routledge.

Shi, W., Sun, L., Yan, D., & Zhu, Z. (2017). Institutional fragility and outward foreign direct investment from China. *Journal of International Business Studies, 48*, 452–476.

Singh, N., & Kundu, S. (2002). Explaining the growth of E-commerce corporations (ECCs): An extension and application of the eclectic paradigm. *Journal of International Business Studies, 33*(4), 679–697. https://doi.org/10.1057/palgrave.jibs.8491039

Sola Gimferrer, P. (2019, 19/7/2019). Las claves del éxito de La casa de papel. *La Vanguardia.* Retrieved from https://www.lavanguardia.com/series/netflix/20190719/463580297705/la-casa-de-papel-claves-exito-serie-netflix.html

Solvell, O., & Birkinshaw, J. (2000). Multinational enterprises and the knowledge economy: Leveraging global practices. In J. Dunning (Ed.), *Regions, globalisation, and the knowledge based economy.* Oxford University Press.

Spagnoletti, P., Resca, A., & Lee, G. (2015). A design theory for digital platforms supporting online communities: A multiple case study. *Journal of Information Technology, 30*, 1. https://doi.org/10.1057/jit.2014.37

Spangler, T. (2021, 16 November 2021). 'Squid Game' Is Decisively Netflix No. 1 Show of All Time With 1.65 Billion Hours Streamed in First Four Weeks, Company Says. *Variety.* Retrieved from https://variety.com/2021/digital/news/squid-game-all-time-most-popular-show-netflix-1235113196/

Stallkamp, M., & Schotter, A. P. (2021). Platforms without borders? The international strategies of digital platform firms. *Global Strategy Journal, 11*(1), 58–80. https://doi.org/10.1002/gsj.1336

Startup Genome. (2022). The global startup ecosystem report. Retrieved from https://startupgenome.com/es/article/the-state-of-the-global-startup-economy

Statista. (2022). E-commerce as percentage of total retail sales worldwide from 2015 to 2021, with forecasts from 2022 to 2026. Retrieved from https://www.statista.com/statistics/534123/e-commerce-share-of-retail-sales-worldwide/

Statista. (2022a). The 100 largest companies in the world by market capitalization in 2022. Retrieved from https://www.statista.com/statistics/263264/top-companies-in-the-world-by-market-capitalization/

Statista. (2022b). GDP Driven by digital transformation 2018–2023. Retrieved from https://www.statista.com/statistics/1134766/nominal-gdp-driven-by-digitally-transformed-enterprises/

Storper, M., & Scott, H. (1995). The wealth of regions. *Futures, 27*(5), 1.

Strange, R., & Zucchella, A. (2017a). Industry 4.0, global value chains and international business. *Multinational Business Review, 25*(4), 1. https://doi. org/10.1108/MBR-05-2017-0028

Strange, R., & Zucchella, A. (2017b). Industry 4.0, global value chains and international business. *Multinational Business Review, 25*(3), 174–184. https://doi.org/10.1108/MBR-05-2017-0028

Suseno, Y., & Pinnington, A. (2018). Building social capital and human capital for internationalization: The role of network ties and knowledge resources. *Asia Pacific Journal of Management, 35*, 1081–1106.

Teece, D., Pisano, G., & Shuen, A. (1997). Dynamic capabilities and strategic management. *Strategic Management Journal, 19*(7), 509–533.

The Economist reporters. (2022, 13/10/2022). China and the West are in a race to foster innovation. *The Economist.*

Thornhill, J. (2018, April 2, 2018). The rise of the information economy threatens traditional companies. *Financial Times.* Retrieved from https://www.ft. com/content/6c6c730e-3298-11e8-ac48-10c6fdc22f03

Thornhill, J. (2021a, 15 July 2021). Technology has ended ownership but can now reinvent it. *Financial Times.*

Thornhill, J. (2021b, 22 April 2021). Technology wars are becoming the new trade wars. *Financial Times.* Retrieved from https://www.ft.com/ content/6fcd69ab-4dcd-4ffa-ae0f-b9aadfc79e52.

Tidd, J., & Bessant, J. (2020). *Managing innovation: Integrating technological, market and organizational change* (7th ed.). Wiley.

Trastulla, L., Noorbakhsh, J., Vazquez, F., McFarland, J., & Iorio, F. (2022). Computational estimation of quality and clinical relevance of cancer cell lines. *Molecular Systems Biology, 18*, 1. https://www.embopress.org/doi/ full/10.15252/msb.202211017.

Trust, G. (2022). Bizarrap & Quevedo's 'Bzrp Music Sessions, Vol. 52' Doubles Up Again Atop Billboard Global Charts. Retrieved from https://finance. yahoo.com/news/bizarrap-quevedo-bzrp-music-sessions-20145 1614.html?guccounter=1&guce_referrer=aHR0cHM6Ly93d3cuZ29v Z2xlLmNvbS8&guce_referrer_sig=AQAAAF56_Trp7z0ar RFR9jANiPPq6Rp7RsUWW0oKY_FLLkyC0yPqy3 ScESa4Rb8XFKjfKFnea0Y4hW0eOrlxWDRlkp5XiUf3pX39NreTFtEPzg 6snTIxMGtANU5G6Gqf2Hti6YjI1WTa5NbvDdlcwXE_dAcw HLbq4xWpYQs4lJChm59w

UNCTAD. (2022). Global foreign direct investment flows over the last 30 years. Retrieved from https://unctad.org/data-visualization/global-foreign-direct-investment-flows-over-last-30-years

Van der Marel, E. (2021). Regulating the globalisation of data: Which model works best? *ECIPE Policy Brief, 9*. Retrieved from https://ecipe.org/wp-content/uploads/2021/05/ECI_21_PolicyBrief_09_2021_LY03.pdf

Vassolo, R., De Castro, J., & Gomez-Mejia, L. (2011). Managing in Latin America: Common issues and a research agenda. *Academy of Management Perspectives, 1*, 22–36.

Verbeke, A., & Lee, I. (2022). *International business strategy. Rethinking the foundations of global corporate success* (3rd ed.). Cambridge University Press.

Vernon, R. (1966). International investment and international trade in the product cycle. *Quarterly Journal of Economics, 80*(2), 190. Retrieved from http://search.epnet.com/login.aspx?direct=true&db=buh&an=4966727

Vernon, R. (1974). The location of economic activity. In J. Dunning (Ed.), *Economic analysis and the multinational Enterprise*. Allen & Unwin.

Vourlias, C. (2021, 18 October 2021). In the Hunt for the Next 'Squid Game,' Industry Execs See 'Unlimited Potential'. *Variety*. Retrieved from https://variety.com/2021/streaming/global/squid-game-netflix-paramount-plus-global-hits-1235091468/

Wang, S. (2018). After years of testing, The Wall Street Journal has built a paywall that bends to the individual reader. Retrieved from https://www.niemanlab.org/2018/02/after-years-of-testing-the-wall-street-journal-has-built-a-paywall-that-bends-to-the-individual-reader/

Weinland, D. (2022, 18/11/2022). The tech war between America and China is just getting started. *The Economist*.

Wesson, T. (1993). *An alternative motivation for foreign direct investment.* Harvard University Press.

Wesson, T. (1997). *A model of asset seeking foreign direct investment.* Paper presented at the The Administration Science Association of Canada.

Williamson, O. (1985). *The economic institutions of capitalism: Firms, markets, relational contracting.* Free Press.

Witt, M. A. (2019). De-globalization: Theories, predictions, and opportunities for international business research. *Journal of International Business Studies, 50*(7), 1053–1077. https://doi.org/10.1057/s41267-019-00219-7

Wolf, M. (2022a, 1 November 2022). Geopolitics is the biggest threat to globalisation. *Financial Times*. Retrieved from https://www.ft.com/content/895 4a5f8-8f03-4044-8401-f1efefe9791b

Wolf, M. (2022b, 13 September 2022). Globalisation is not dying, it's changing. *Financial Times*. Retrieved from https://www.ft.com/content/f6fe91ab-39f9-44b0-bff6-505ff6c665a1

Word Economic Forum. (2022). These are the top 10 job skills of tomorrow – and how long it takes to learn them. Retrieved from https://www.weforum. org/agenda/2020/10/top-10-work-skills-of-tomorrow-how-long-it-takes-to-learn-them/

Wright, M., Filatotchev, I., Hoskisson, R. E., & Peng, M. W. (2005). Strategy research in emerging economies: Challenging the conventional wisdom. *Journal of Management Studies, 42*(1), 1–33.

WTO. (2013). *The general agreement on trade in services.* WTO Trade in Services Division.

WTO. (2017a). WTO, World Economic Forum and eWTP launch joint public-private dialogue to open up e-commerce for small business. Retrieved from https://www.wto.org/english/news_e/news17_e/ecom_11dec17_e.htm

WTO. (2017b). *Trade facilitation agreement.* World Trade Organisation.

WTO. (2019). Joint Initiative on E-commerce [Press release]. Retrieved from https://www.wto.org/english/tratop_e/ecom_e/joint_statement_e.htm

WTO. (2022). Statistics on trade in commercial services. Retrieved from https://www.wto.org/english/res_e/statis_e/tradeserv_stat_e.htm

Xuemei, X., Yuhang, H., Alistair, A., & Samuel, R.-N. (2022). Digital platforms and SMEs' business model innovation: Exploring the mediating mechanisms of capability reconfiguration. *International Journal of Information Management, 65,* 102513. https://doi.org/10.1016/j.ijinfomgt.2022. 102513

Yablonsky, S. (2018). Transaction platforms: Fintech platforms. In *Multi-sided platforms (MSPs) and sharing strategies in the digital economy: Emerging research and opportunities* (pp. 113–133). Hershey, PA, USA.

Yin, J., Li, F., Lu, Y., Zeng, S., & Zhu, F. (2021). Identification of the key target profiles underlying the drugs of narrow therapeutic index for treating cancer and cardiovascular disease. *Computational and Structural Biotechnology Journal, 19,* 2318–2328.

Yogesh, K. D., Laurie, H., Elvira, I., Gert, A., Crispin, C., Tom, C., et al. (2021). Artificial intelligence (AI): Multidisciplinary perspectives on emerging challenges, opportunities, and agenda for research, practice and policy. *International Journal of Information Management, 57,* 101994. https://doi. org/10.1016/j.ijinfomgt.2019.08.002

Zaheer, S. (1995). Overcoming the liability of foreignness. *Academy of Management Journal, 38*(2), 341–363.

Zeng, M., & Williamson, J. (2003). The hidden dragons *Harvard Business Review, October 2003,* 92–99.

Zheng, N., & Qu, Y. (2015). What explains the performance of Chinese exporting firms? *Journal of Chinese Economic and Business Studies, 13*(1), 51–70.

Zhou, L. (2007). The effects of entrepreneurial proclivity and foreign market knowledge on early internationalization. *Journal of World Business, 42*, 281–293.

簡睿哲, Jean, B. R.-J., Kim, D., Zhou, K. Z., & Cavusgil, S. T. (2021). E-Platform use and exporting in the context of Alibaba: A signaling theory perspective. *Journal of International Business Studies*. Retrieved from http://nccur.lib.nccu.edu.tw/handle/140.119/135880.

Index[1]

---

[1] Note: Page numbers followed by 'n' refer to notes.

GPSR Compliance
The European Union's (EU) General Product Safety Regulation (GPSR) is a set
of rules that requires consumer products to be safe and our obligations to
ensure this.

If you have any concerns about our products, you can contact us on

ProductSafety@springernature.com

In case Publisher is established outside the EU, the EU authorized
representative is:

Springer Nature Customer Service Center GmbH
Europaplatz 3
69115 Heidelberg, Germany